As I read this book, two wor[ds kept coming to mind:] "words." From the late 1840[s, faithful Saints began to] petition a change in the exclusionary and harmful policy that denied priesthood ordination to Blacks. In 1973, those prayers were joined by the words of Lester Bush, whose landmark article in *Dialogue: A Journal of Mormon Thought* helped pry open the door to the 1978 revelation. Countless prayers have gone up to petition changes in the church's LGBTQ+ policies and doctrines, and now *Queer Mormon Theology* adds words to those prayers—perhaps the right words to pry open yet another door.

—Gregory A. Prince
Author of *Gay Rights and the Mormon Church: Intended Actions, Unintended Consequences*

For most members of the Church of Jesus Christ of Latter-day Saints, its theology is only ever viewed through the authorized lens of Church Correlation.

In *Queer Mormon Theology*, author Blaire Ostler offers a fresh look at the basic tenets of the religion as seen through the eyes of a queer church member.

The discoveries she reveals may surprise, captivate, and simultaneously invite the reader to explore new perspectives on living and worshiping as an inclusive community of Saints.

—Laurie Lee Hall
Architect

Blaire Ostler's considerate work offers new perspectives around old questions of gender and relationships that have long plagued the larger Mormon community. As Latter-day Saints explore the meaning of discipleship in a modern world, Ostler extends a roadmap of true Christian living and Grace that is big and wide enough to embrace more of God's children in faith, love and inclusion. Readers will come to engage the Gospel in a way that liberates rather than oppresses. She eloquently demonstrates how to nurture faith and subsume a more holistic relationship with the Divine, where the only sacrifice required is leaving pride at the door and opening one's heart to more love, light and wisdom.

—Lindsay Hansen Park
Executive director of the Sunstone Education Foundation
and host of the *Year of Polygamy* podcast

By Common Consent Press is a non-profit publisher dedicated to producing affordable, high-quality books that help define and shape the Latter-day Saint experience. BCC Press publishes books that address all aspects of Mormon life. Our mission includes finding manuscripts that will contribute to the lives of thoughtful Latter-day Saints, mentoring authors and nurturing projects to completion, and distributing important books to the Mormon audience at the lowest possible cost.

QUEER MORMON THEOLOGY

AN INTRODUCTION

BLAIRE OSTLER

Queer Mormon Theology: An Introduction
Copyright © 2021 by Blaire Ostler

All rights reserved. Printed in the United States of America. No part of this book may be used or reproduced in any manner whatsoever without written permission except in the case of brief quotations embodied in critical articles or reviews.

For information contact
By Common Consent Press
4900 Penrose Dr.
Newburgh, IN 47630

Cover design: D Christian Harrison
Book design: Andrew Heiss

www.bccpress.org
ISBN-13: 978-1-948218-41-2

10 9 8 7 6 5 4 3 2 1

for God's queer children

Contents

Foreword		ix
Introduction		1
1	Concerning Theology	7
2	Concerning God	21
3	Concerning Christ	37
4	Concerning The Family	49
5	Concerning Sexuality and Creation	63
6	Concerning Polygamy	77
7	Concerning Policy	95
	Afterword: Concerning the Beehive	117
	Acknowledgements	121
	Notes	123

Foreword

In January of 2015, I stood in an upper room of the Brooklyn Borough Hall in New York City to see the St. Francis of Assisi exhibition. I was surrounded by beautifully illuminated, handwritten eight-hundred-year-old documents of Catholic governance and worship from the period of St. Francis.

While at the exhibit, Dr. John Edwards from St. Francis College gave a short lecture about St. Francis, the Franciscan order, and their place in church history. He taught that for two thousand years, the Catholic Church went through cycles of decline and renewal. During periods of decline, saving monastic and mendicant orders, such as the Franciscans, rose from outside the church hierarchy to lead the church away from its intimate relationship with politics and wealth, and to forsake the corrupt policies and practices that accompany such relationships.

As I left the exhibit, I reflected on our own history as a young church—our own cycles of decline and renewal, crisis and change. I specifically thought about the current crisis centering on rejecting behavior towards queer Latter-day Saints. How do we reconcile a restored theology majestically rising on the world from First Vision to King Follett—fueled by prophetic promise that "Our Heavenly Father is more liberal in his views, and boundless in his mercies and blessings, than we are ready to believe or receive"—with policies and practices rooted in prejudice, harassment, and discrimination that have structured the everyday life of queer Latter-day Saints for generations?

Much of my work as president of Affirmation: LGBTQ Mormons, Families & Friends occurs within the aftermath of such policies and practices. Affirmation confidently stands in the intersection of Queer/Latter-day Saint life and responds to the calls of our queer peers from the margins, rushing to render aid and build communities of safety, love, and hope. Our work is both immediate and practical: providing a healing and supportive community of queer mentors who not only help contextualize policies and practices, but affirm and empower each queer soul as they claim their space to confidently and authentically stand in places that feel safe and healthy for them.

From my work in the margins, it becomes clear that policies and practices have been utilized over the generations to contort and break queer bodies to fit a dominant narrative about our theology that simply isn't true. It cannot be sustained, for that narrative only works if queer people are marginalized and erased. Why would our Heavenly Parents do that to anyone? Who are we to restrict the margins when Jesus accessed the margins?

It is here in this moment, much like St. Francis, that Blaire steps in and immediately discards the problematic dominant narrative that manages queer bodies in the church. She turns our attention to the theology of restoration and renewal that has always been with us. She lifts our chin and invites us to walk with her as she expertly shows us that in the absence of prejudice and folk tradition, there is not a significant difference between queer Mormon theology and Mormon theology.

To see queer theology hidden in plain sight, Blaire invites us all to do a hard thing. She asks those who may not identify as queer to suspend prejudices and misconceptions about sexual orientation, gender identity, and gender expression and see that the familiar theology in the Church of Jesus Christ of Latter-day Saints is inherently inclusive of our queer siblings. To those in the queer community she asks us to be a bit vulnerable and allow ourselves the grace to see the familiar theology stripped of policies and practices, where Jesus is not wiping away our queerness, but is instead the Christ who experiences queerness with us.

I can think of no one better to introduce queer Mormon theology at this moment than Blaire Ostler. She is a published poet and accomplished scholar in both the fine arts and philosophy, the kind of contemporary thinker who can skillfully connect great ideas that appear to be in conflict. Over the years, in her publications, presentations, podcasts, and personal writings, Blaire has given us a window into her brilliant mind and thoughtful philosophy. And like all great teachers, she has then invited us to expand our own horizons as we look towards self, families, community, and to the heavens.

But this is not all. To queer a familiar phrase: "Queer philosophy, if it hath not works, is dead, being alone." Blaire couples her powerful ideas and thoughts with her work in queer spaces. For example, she is always extremely generous with her time in building queer communities, such as Affirmation and QueerMeals. She has stood outside the Conference Center with her queer peers, inviting members to stop for a moment and "Hug a Queer Mormon," hugging so many conference goers as to lose count. Most importantly, although she would never reveal this herself, I can attest that she spends hours sitting with her queer peers, bearing burdens, and lifting the hands that hang down.

It is this combination of both philosophy and practice that makes her ideas fresh and exciting, as well as uplifting and healing. It is this combination that reveals wisdom. Therefore, her thesis that "inclusion of queer Latter-day Saints within modern orthopraxy is the natural consequence of our robust theology" is grounded in both insight and charity. This puts her in the unique position to write this book at this moment in our cycle of queer relations within the church.

Queer people have always been with us since the beginnings of the Restoration, yet until recently we have not seen them. In the church's two-hundred-year history, queer people have continually blessed us, but we have not recognized it. And because we have not recognized them, we have not seen the spaces in our theology that queerness occupies. The hope and beauty of Blaire's words in *Queer Mormon Theology: An Introduction* begin to rectify this situation in a way that not only lifts God's queer children, but lifts us all. As you begin Blaire's book, consider these words from a queer perspective, the end of a poem I wrote several years ago, that speak to the life-giving importance of recognizing queer Mormons in the theology of the Restoration.

> We will always be with you, see us!
> We continually wash upon your shores as waves,
> Born to our families to bless you
> When you did not realize you were in need of blessing.
>
> And the blessing of waves shapes shorelines,
> And tides bring life
> To the everlasting lands
> Of the Kingdom of God.

—Nathan Kitchen
President, Affirmation: LGBTQ Mormons, Families & Friends

Introduction

President Dieter F. Uchtdorf of The Church of Jesus Christ of Latter-day Saints stated emphatically, across a neatly polished pulpit, "There is room for you in this church."¹ I listened attentively as he continued: "Regardless of your circumstances, your personal history, or the strength of your testimony, there is room for you in this church." I desperately wanted these words to be true. Was there really room in the church for a someone like me?

Growing up as a queer Mormon in The Church of Jesus Christ of Latter-day Saints, I had few resources and role models I could turn to for help with my uniquely queer experience. Any vulnerability I expressed, which wasn't much, was met with ignorance, disgust, or rejection. Though I didn't have the words to adequately describe my sexual orientation, gender experience, or biology, I knew I was experiencing things that were atypical—or, better stated, queer. Even though I was young with a limited understanding of queer issues, I knew that "queer" meant something bad. I was sure that I wasn't bad; therefore, I reasoned, I couldn't be queer. It didn't occur to me that, despite all the voices telling me that being queer was bad, being queer could be something beautiful—even godly.

Today, I proudly identify as a queer Mormon. I'm a born-and-raised Mormon, brought up in The Church of Jesus Christ of Latter-day Saints. To this day, I still hold to my Mormon beliefs, testimony, doctrine, theology, culture, and heritage. I come from nine generations of Mormon pioneers. I often joke that, if there is a Mormon gene, I have it. I also often joke that, if there is a queer gene, I have it too. I sometimes get negative reactions from people inside and outside of the Church for not relinquishing one or the other of these identities. They sometimes insist that a person couldn't possibly be both queer and Mormon, especially given the Church's history of painful attempts to delegitimize the queer community. It is easy to understand why some would be skeptical about the possibility of someone being queer and Mormon. Even so, I maintain that I am a queer Mormon.

While some books on queer Mormonism center on the Church as the protagonist, this book does the opposite. This book centers the queer experience within Mormonism and explores the ways that the Church can adapt to the queerness of our theology. If Mormonism has the truth, then we must gather up the bits of truth that sit on the outskirts of our pews and usher them into the fold. As Joseph Smith stated, "Mormonism is truth; and every man who embraces it feels himself at liberty to embrace every truth: consequently the shackles of superstition, bigotry, ignorance, and priestcraft, fall at once from his neck; and his eyes are opened to see the truth."[2] In the spirit of Mormonism, I have a truth to share, and that truth is queer.

Our theology has a long history of adaptations (e.g., polygamy, race, etc.). Mormonism, like all living organisms, must learn to adapt in order to survive. Mormonism's ability to adapt to and accommodate new truths and new perspectives cannot be overstated. I see no reason to believe that Mormonism will not continue to accommodate new truths as they make themselves evident. This book is one way to make queer experiences visible so that Mormons can incorporate the truth of these experiences into a worldview that harmonizes all truth into one great gospel.

This might be a jarring text to read because it centers the queer Latter-day Saint experience through affirmation. This book affirms that the queer Mormon experience is as legitimate and godly as the non-queer experience. "Mormon" and "queer" are not mutually exclusive categories. Both live inside me.

Another reason this book might be jarring for readers is that it is blasphemy to the silos which separate the academic from the personal, the pastoral from the scientific, and the prophetic from the historical. This book is an interweaving of my personal experience, academic expertise, scientific inquiry, theological exploration, and pastoral invitations and proclamations. After all, how could the journal of my life be anything less when the flesh of my body and the expression of my soul were turned into an academic project, scientific experiment, and a source of eternal damnation? This book offers a mosaic composed of the shattered dreams of a broken theology repaired and resurrected by a queer Mormon looking for her promised divinity. I am putting queerness in the center of the stage, shining a spotlight down on her, and handing her a microphone to sing an unheard song. From the pulpit, in conference meetings, or in handbooks, my existence challenges the Mormon imagination to see beyond binaries and false claims of eternally fixed identities. My existence is fluid and bleeds through the cracks of a porous ontology. For these reasons, I acknowledge that many will find this book jarring and even disorienting—because that's exactly what it is. Queerness challenges limited views of Mormonism and invites us all to see it as an already existing aspect of our theology.

As I listen to my own daughter tell me about her dreams of marrying a girl, I cannot help but yearn for a better theology for our queer children. After all, a queer mother is still a mother. Our queer children and youth deserve better than what their queer parents received. Make no mistake, while I preach a theology of queer inclusivity, Mormon history and discourse have caused significant harm and trauma to the queer community. I want the trauma to end—yes, for myself, but even more so for our children. We should not burden our children with the sins and traumas of their parents.

I believe we can repair the trauma done to the queer community. We must heal together. Whether any of us like it or not, queer people are not going away, and every day, queer kids are born into the Church. Their health and safety should be our primary concern. Is there room for them in the Church? I want to believe that there is, but the truth of Elder Uchtdorf's comment depends on our ability to make room for people who sit on the margins. Healing must be a communal endeavor. Atonement is a journey, and it begins with a belief in the possibility that there is room for queer folks in the Church. And this means more than just inclusive policies. While I agree that policy is important, changing policy without revising theology is an empty gesture. Policy reflects theology. For policies to improve and stick, they must be within the bounds of our theology.

As I have grown in both faith and understanding, I have come to see that Mormon theology is inherently queer. It wasn't obvious at first, but now I can't see it any other way. From scriptural narratives to polygamous pioneers, we are a queer and peculiar people. The phrase "peculiar people" is originally found in the King James Version of the Bible and used as a descriptor for "God's people."[3] The phrase is also a common way for Mormons to describe themselves. Many Mormons take pride in their peculiarity, and what is "peculiar" but another way to say "queer"? The richness of Mormon theology cannot be reduced to something non-queer, at least not in any simplistic sense. Mormon theology holds the building blocks for an orthodoxy of love and inclusion beyond what is discussed in Sunday school.

The discovery of a queer orthodoxy requires our participation. Queer Mormon theology is written by those willing to write, spoken by those willing to speak, read by those willing to read, and heard by those willing to listen. It can only be accepted by those willing to accept. This is how continuing revelation works. Continuing revelation is not a task reserved for an elite group of apostles. It is an ongoing process implemented by those seeking to improve themselves and their world. Continuing revelation is the percolation of powerful ideas through a robust network of individuals and influences. We embody continuing revelation. I now see the beautiful queerness of our theology, and I hope that, through this book, others will too.

This book is not meant as a stagnant set of unquestionable dictates, but rather as a step toward the fluid exploration of how the queer community belongs in Mormon theology. I believe in continuing revelation and that the Restoration is still happening. I accept and welcome both academic and theological improvements and adaptations to my work—especially from my queer peers. I hope that in the future a fellow queer scholar will read this book and be inspired to create something better by sharing their queer Mormon experience too.

While I do not expect this sentiment to be received easily or without ridicule from the gatekeepers of orthodoxy and other religious critics, I believe I have been called to do this work. I'm confident that I will do it imperfectly. I trust that I will commit errors in judgment and that there will be others who expand upon my work and make it even more beautiful and powerful than I can currently imagine. I trust that in time even my own views, semantics, terminology, and ideas concerning gender, sexuality, science, and theology will change. However, I believe I am called by the Spirit to do this work to the best of my abilities and to share the queer gospel of Christ through Mormon theology. My entire life has prepared me for this work.

It is with epistemic humility that I do not speak directly to issues of race within the queer experience. I am limited by my experience as a white person, and it is not my place to tell a story that isn't mine. However, the intersection of queerness and race in Mormonism is important and needs to be addressed. Those who share their lived experiences as queer Mormons of color deserve our attention. I do my best to share my queer experience, philosophy, and theology with the understanding that my experience cannot be universally applied to all queer members. I simply offer my experience among many as I attempt to articulate the most inclusive theology that I can.

I want to unequivocally state my position to the queer Mormon community: my work is not a prescription for queer Mormons. It would be unfair of me to ask you to share my optimism about the current political climate of the Church. We are experiencing the growing pains of a young religion. Queer folks are not sincerely welcomed and affirmed in the Church at this time—I acknowledge that. I am not here to tell you how to live your life. Each queer person is different, and my path will not be your path. I trust we are all doing the best we can to process overwhelming and conflicting messages, suggestions, and commands from every possible vantage point concerning our queerness. I'm here to tell you I love you, and I believe your queerness is a godly part of who you are. That is all. What you do with your divine nature is up to you.

This book is broken into seven chapters that cover core tenants of queer Mormon theology. The first chapter covers the basics of terminology and our theological responsibility to be deliberate participants. The second chapter tells the story of God from a queer perspective; God is far more inclusive, expansive, and queer in our theology than we have accounted for. The third chapter discusses Jesus Christ and our active role as members of the body of Christ. In this chapter, I bring to light how we are made queer in Christ. The fourth chapter addresses concerns with *The Family: A Proclamation to the World*. The fifth chapter lays out various ways that queer families might create in the eternities. Eternal increase, creation, and progression is not a process reserved for cisgender heterosexuals. The sixth chapter addresses polygamy and its queerness. The seventh and final chapter offers next steps and solutions to make our policies, pews, temples, rituals, and eternities queer-inclusive. A brief afterword speaks directly to queer Mormons as we persist in our labors to legitimize ourselves with Mormonism.

For those who are reading this book, my hope is that together we can make Elder Uchtdorf's words true. I see a future where the pews of Latter-day Saint chapels are filled with queer kids, couples, and families fully welcomed as worthy participants. I have seen such a beautiful image of the future in my mind that I cannot help but do my part to bring it to fruition. This book is one step toward a future where we can truly say to queer Saints, "There is room for you in this church."

CHAPTER 1

Concerning Theology

To have queer-inclusive policies, we need to first examine our theology. In my youth, I was taught some harmful folk doctrines about what celestial bodies and families would be like. I was taught that brown and black bodies would become lighter. I was taught that intersex bodies would be corrected. I was taught that gay, lesbian, and bisexual bodies would no longer desire members of the same sex and that trans folks would have their gender identity taken from them. I was taught that queerness was a sin in the eyes of God and that no such queerness would exist in the presence of God. These folk theologies have caused significant suffering among queer Latter-day Saints. I know because I used to be one of the many Latter-day Saints who believed that there wasn't room for me in celestial eternities.

As I grew into adulthood, it became evident that this interpretation of theology was severely lacking, even harmful. Eventually, I learned that there was more than one way to understand Mormon theology. Mormonism not only had room for queerness but is inherently queer itself. As adherents of Mormon theology, we must be held accountable for the harm being done and to do better moving forward. It is our theological responsibility to dive into the richness of Mormon theology and uncover the queerness within.

Clarifying Queer

Throughout the book, you will find the word "queer" used in multiple ways. (1) I use "queer" as an umbrella term for those in the LGBTQIA+ community; (2) I use "queer" as a personal identity label; and (3) I use "queer" to describe the peculiarity of God's people.

First, I use the term "queer" as an umbrella term for those in the LGBTQIA+ community. As a matter of practicality, it is easier to say the queer community than to list all the various and ever-changing labels under the queer umbrella of sexual orientations and gender identities. Each letter is important and serves a purpose. Adding letters has been a necessary and helpful evolution to include members of the queer community who are something other than gay or lesbian. We should continue to add more letters as we learn more about gender, sex, and sexuality. However, LGBTQIA+ is a mouthful. "Queer" is only one syllable. It's more efficient when referring to the entire community as "queer" rather than list out each individual letter. Queer, in this context, simply means something other than cisgender and/or heterosexual.

Second, I use the word "queer" as a personal self-identifier. I'm bisexual, or pansexual, which means that I experience sexual attraction and desire towards a diversity of genders. I like all genders, and my romantic and sexual interests are more concerned with who a person is rather than their pronouns or gender performance. I am also biologically queer with intersex characteristics which contribute to the queerness of my gender experience. The term "queer" has become a comfortable identifier for the experience of being a sexually fluid, gender variant woman. In short, I like what I like when I like it. I am who I am, and that person is always changing. It's queer.

I was once approached by a Latter-day Saint woman who asked me why I would call myself "queer." She was genuinely perplexed and wanted to know why I would identify with a label that was considered derogatory. She said, "When I was growing up, queer was a bad thing." Her confusion was understandable. Growing up, I heard the label "queer" used in a derogatory manner as well, even by my family. I rationalized that I wasn't really "queer," and they weren't really talking about me. If "queer" means bad, I reasoned, then that can't be me because I'm not bad.

I explained to the woman that embracing the label "queer" is an act of redemption. I am queer, and that's not bad. Call me queer. It's who I am. There is no shame in my queerness. As demonstrated by Queer Nation, founded in 1990, the term "queer" has been reclaimed as a positive term.[1] More recently, the word has been adopted by academic communities as well.[2] I'm queer and unashamed.

Respecting a person's label is not simply a matter of civil niceties or politeness; it is a matter of respecting one's autonomy as a self-determining agent. To label an experience, such as the queer experience, is to confer dignity upon those who wear the label. It is the legitimization of a lived experience. To erase someone's self-conferred label strips a person of their autonomy as a free agent. This is particularly important to transgender and non-binary folks who must continually work to legitimize their self-identification in ways most people take for granted.

However, identity is more than self-identification. It's also about recognition within a community. No one is an island, and we formulate identities in a symbiotic process of becoming. When my queer predecessors died over the label "queer," it wasn't just about legitimizing semantics. It was about recognizing and legitimizing an idea, which included semantics. The queer community said, "I'm queer, and that's not bad." The other half of the equation is whether the rest of the community is willing to respect our identification. Identity is both an inward and outward experience.

If you are non-queer and wonder if you can use the word "queer," the answer is yes. Like all words, the way you use it matters. So when you use the word "queer," ask yourself, "Am I putting the queer community down or lifting the queer community up?" Granted, some members of the queer community struggle with the reclamation of the word "queer." If your gay friend doesn't like being called "queer," then don't do it. Generally, though, the reclamation of the word "queer" is gaining steam and popularity both inside and outside the queer community.

Another reason I have adopted the label "queer" is that it affords privacy. Queer signifies an experience that is outside the cisgender and/or heterosexual experience without divulging too many details. This can be refreshing for people who would like to be "out" about their queerness without having to list their sexual preference, history, medical treatments, transitional procedures, or other personal information. A constant struggle for social acceptance is balancing privacy with legitimacy. For example, to legitimize gay marriage, people will need to "come out." Sexual preferences are private and intimate information. Yet, to legalize and legitimize gay marriage, people would have to make their desires to be married to their same-sex partner known or "out." For many of us, legitimacy and privacy are constantly competing with one another. The label "queer" affords a balance of both.

Third, I use the word "queer" interchangeably with the word "peculiar." Queer is anything strange, odd, or atypical. I find the term particularly relevant for Mormons and Latter-day Saints who often take pride in our peculiarity. The holy nation of God is a peculiar one indeed. In Peter we read, "But ye are a chosen generation, a royal priesthood, a holy nation, a peculiar people; that ye should shew forth the praises of him who hath called you out of darkness into his marvelous light: Which in time past were not a people but are now the people of God."[3] God's people are a peculiar people, and as we fully embrace our diversity in the body of Christ, we will find we are also a queer people. In this sense, I use the word "queer" to embrace the peculiarity of the people of God.

Clarifying Mormon

In the October 2018 General Conference, President Russell M. Nelson gave strong remarks concerning the name of the Church and the term "Mormon." He stated, "Some weeks ago, I released a statement regarding a course correction for the name of the Church. I did this because the Lord impressed upon my mind the importance of the name He decreed for His Church, even The Church of Jesus Christ of Latter-day Saints."[4] He continued to list several nicknames that the Church has been known by and encouraged members to not use names that remove Christ from the focus of the Church. He stated, "To remove the Lord's name from the Lord's Church is a major victory for Satan."[5]

Further in his remarks, he notes that, in the early formation of the Church, the term "Mormon" was a derogatory term. He states, "In the early days of the restored Church, terms such as Mormon Church and Mormons were often used as epithets—as cruel terms, abusive terms—designed to obliterate God's hand in restoring the Church of Jesus Christ in these latter days." Nelson's remarks, in conjunction with the Church style guide, encourage members of the Church to generally abandon the term "Mormon." I say "generally" because the term "Mormonism" is found in our scriptures and cannot be fully rejected.

In Doctrine and Covenants, the term "Mormonism" is used in high esteem. John Taylor referred to the martyrdom of Joseph Smith as a "broad seal affixed to Mormonism." The full scripture reads, "They were innocent of any crime, as they had often been proved before, and were only confined in jail by the conspiracy of traitors and wicked men; and their innocent blood on the floor of Carthage jail is a broad seal affixed to 'Mormonism' that cannot be rejected by any court on earth."[6]

Joseph Smith himself used the term "Mormonism" to denote truth. In his words, "Hell may pour forth its rage like the burning lava of Mount Vesuvius, or of Etna, or of the most terrible of the burning mountains; and yet shall 'Mormonism' stand. Water, fire, truth and God are all realities. Truth is 'Mormonism.'"[7] Joseph Smith did not cower to his oppressor's use of the term "Mormon." He embraced the term and wore it with honor. Joseph Smith associated "Mormonism" with the "grand fundamental principles" and encouraged the Saints to be "true Mormons." In his words, ". . . we should gather up all the good and true principles in the world and treasure them up, or we shall not come out true 'Mormons.'"[8] Joseph repeatedly used the term "Mormon" in a positive way and encouraged followers to live up to the name "Mormon."

President Nelson's remarks are in stark contrast to Joseph Smith and our scriptures. While Nelson may rightfully counsel Latter-day Saints to use the correct full name of the Church, the term "Mormon" cannot be so easily abandoned when it is written in our scriptures. Not only that, "Mormon" is used to denote truth by our founder and among early Saints.

Prior to Nelson's talk, President Gordon B. Hinckley gave a conference talk in 1990 which addressed this very issue. In his talk, he echoed Joseph Smith's esteem for the word "Mormon." Hinckley suggested that "Mormon" is nothing to be ashamed of. In fact, it means "more good."[9] In his talk, President Hinckley agrees that the name of the Church is non-negotiable. However, he speaks up on behalf of the term "Mormon" as worthy of redemption.

I concur with what past and present presidents have said about the name of the Church being non-negotiable. The name is written in our scriptures, "Thus shall my church be called in the last days, even The Church of Jesus Christ of Latter-day Saints."[10] However, "Mormonism" is also written in scripture. Abandoning the term is not simply a matter of inconvenience, as Nelson suggests—it is contrary to Latter-day Saint scripture.[11] If it were simply a matter of inconvenience, we could persevere, but inconvenience is not the issue at hand. The Church is founded on the principles of Mormonism—not just by nickname, but by sacred doctrine. Both the name of the Church and the sacredness of Mormonism is written in our scripture.

The title of this book might be difficult for some to embrace when it contains the terms "queer" and "Mormon." As noted in the previous section, the term "queer" has similar roots to the term "Mormon" in that both were intended to be derogatory terms but have since been embraced as positive terms by those who they intended to hurt. Granted, the reclamation process for both terms has not always been unanimous, but terminology usage rarely, if ever, is unanimous.

It is also worth noting that "Mormonism" is a term used by other denominations, not simply The Church of Jesus Christ of Latter-day Saints. Joseph Smith didn't just spur the formation of our church but also gave rise to many other churches and sects within the Mormon tradition. The Church doesn't own the term "Mormon," legally or socially. It is bigger than any single sect. The use of the term "Mormon" in this book is not an indication of members of The Church of Jesus Christ of Latter-day Saints, but a term used to indicate those who identify as Mormon. A person can be both a Latter-day Saint and a Mormon; they are not mutually exclusive labels.

In this book, I use the term "Mormon" with great respect and admiration for all those who identify as such. "Mormonism" is nothing shameful for Mormons, just as "queerness" is nothing shameful for the queer community. Simultaneously, I adhere to the request of President Nelson to call the Church by its full and proper name and use the approved shorthand term "the Church" thereafter.[12]

It is important to do our best to respect identity labels, and the queer community knows this better than most. On many occasions, the Church has disregarded our labels in favor of more dehumanizing labels, such as "those who struggle with same-gender attraction" instead of "gay," "lesbian," "bisexual," or "queer."[13] I have had many instances where fellow Latter-day Saints refused to call me "queer" because they considered it offensive. Similarly, transgender members have often been denied their correct names and pronouns. In this book, I do my best to respect the style guide approved by President Nelson, use the term "Mormon" with high esteem like Joseph Smith, and hope that in return, Latter-day Saints grant us the same courtesy. Any mistakes I make hereafter are unintentional.

Queer Mormon Theology

There isn't a significant difference between queer Mormon theology and Mormon theology. Queer Mormon theology might even be redundant. Queer Mormon theology simply brings to light the queerness hidden in plain sight. However, considering the current climate, queer Mormon theology is needed to demonstrate its inherent queerness.

In his book *Radical Love*, queer theologian Patrick S. Cheng, outlines the foundations of theology. He lists four sources (1) scriptures, (2) tradition, (3) reason, and (4) experience.[14] I have used his model as a template for my own theological development, with one addition. In Latter-day experience, the Holy Ghost plays a significant role in confirming what is right and wrong, so much so that the Spirit requires its own category.[15] President Joseph Fielding Smith taught, "Through the Holy Ghost the truth is woven into the very fiber and sinews of the body so that it cannot be forgotten."[16] For our purposes, I will add a fifth category to Cheng's model, (5) the Holy Spirit.

These five categories offer a system of checks and balances, where a person can compare scripture with tradition, or reason with the Spirit, or tradition with experience. Theology is not bound to any single category. Depending on the situation, there could be a time when reason and experience override tradition. Some situations require we rely heavily upon reason, while other times we must rely heavily upon the Spirit. It is not my intention to prescribe one source of theology as more important than another in all situations for all people. However, I do suggest that each of us introspectively evaluate how we develop our own interpretations of theology and how we might improve.

1. Scripture

Developing theology relies upon scripture. Scripture, broadly defined, is a sacred text communally accepted by a religious group. Mormon scripture includes the Old and New Testaments, the Book of Mormon, the Doctrine and Covenants, and The Pearl of Great Price—collectively, these scriptures are called the Standard Works.

Latter-day Saints may debate whether other texts should be included as scripture, such as specific conference talks, proclamations, music, sermons, poetry, or texts. For example, I consider Joseph Smith's "King Follet Sermon" to be doctrine, while another Latter-day Saint may not. Another may consider the *A Family: A Proclamation to the World* to be doctrine, while I do not. Regardless of anyone's personal experiences, we cannot deny that these texts and others play an important role in Mormon theology and ritual. Moreover, it is not my intent to argue that texts outside the Standard Works are or are not doctrine—only that we might consider them under the umbrella of texts that have influenced Mormon theology.

2. Tradition

Theology draws heavily upon tradition. This is especially true for Mormon theology. Mormons and Latter-day Saints make strong claims about prophets being on the earth today to guide and direct us toward eternal life. Apostles, prophets, pastors, teachers, evangelists, and so forth all have significant influence in the development of Mormon theology.[17]

It is also important to keep in mind that Joseph Smith taught that a prophet is only a prophet when acting as such.[18] Prophets are fallible. It would be unfair to them, and us, to expect perfection from an imperfect being. This is one reason why we have the gift of personal revelation to discern when a prophet is acting as a prophet. In a very real sense, we are all apostles, prophets, pastors, teachers, and evangelists—when we act as such. Whether by God's voice or by the voice of

God's servants, it is the same.[19] This is exactly what priesthood power is in Mormonism—the power to act in the name of God. May we all act in the name of God and prophesy according to the Spirit. May we all be prophets using priesthood power to bring forth visions of our divine potential.

In Doctrine and Covenants we read, "And all things shall be done by common consent in the church, by much prayer and faith, for all things you shall receive by faith."[20] This means the creation of the Mormon tradition is, and has always been, a communal endeavor. Continuing revelation is the percolation of powerful ideas through a robust network of individuals and influences. May we all embody continuing revelation as we create the Mormon tradition.

3. Reason

Reason is an essential component of understanding theology. With advancements in science, we are gaining a more comprehensive understanding of human biology, anatomy, and gender. Secular arguments against the queer community are often advanced with the claim that "it's unnatural," but we can study the natural world and see a broad range of diverse gender variations, adaptations, and sexual behaviors. The natural world is full of queerness.[21] However, though queerness can be found in the natural world, "natural" is not tantamount to "moral." We must use reason to decipher morality beyond "naturalness." As Mormons, we need to embrace new knowledge and aspects of truth wherever they come from, and this includes reason.

George Q. Cannon wrote that Prophet Joseph Smith "loved learning." He continued, "He loved knowledge for its righteous power. [. . .] The Lord had commanded him to study, and he was obeying. His mind, quickened by the Holy Spirit, grasped with readiness all true principles, and one by one he mastered these branches and became in them a teacher."[22] It is in this balance of reason and spirit that Latter-day Saints might gain a better understanding of our existence. Joseph Smith himself wrote,

> Mormonism is truth, in other words the doctrine of the Latter-day Saints, is truth. . . . The first and fundamental principle of our holy religion is, that we believe that we have a right to embrace all, and every item of truth, without limitation or without being

circumscribed or prohibited by the creeds or superstitious notions of men, or by the dominations of one another, when that truth is clearly demonstrated to our minds, and we have the highest degree of evidence of the same.[23]

I particularly like that Joseph Smith unequivocally stated that we should embrace every item of truth without limitation. If we want truth, we must pursue it. The phrase "search, ponder, and pray" cannot neglect searching as a necessary part of finding truth.[24] Whether truth comes from science, religion, reason, logic, or the Spirit, according to the Mormon tradition, we should seek after it and embrace it.

4. Experience

The lived experiences of queer folks should not be overlooked in the development of Mormon theology. Our experiences are just as godly as any other's, and the neglect or condemnation of our experience is causing harm—real, tangible, physical harm to the queer Mormon community. We must, at the very least, listen to the experiences of queer Mormons if we are ever going to have a more inclusive vision of Mormon theology. As so aptly stated by Elder Russell M. Ballard, "We need to listen to and understand what our LGBT brothers and sisters are feeling and experiencing. Certainly, we must do better than we have done in the past so that all members feel they have a spiritual home where their brothers and sisters love them and where they have a place to worship and serve the Lord."[25]

Listening to queer experiences is the first step to understanding. If we write off queer experiences without listening, we have cut off the promise of continuing revelation. God cannot override our agency and reveal to us what we would not accept or would willingly deny. As the Prophet Joseph Smith noted, "When God offers a blessing or knowledge to a man, and he refuses to receive it, he will be damned."[26] We must be open to understanding experiences outside our own.

Christ experienced queerness with me in the Garden of Gethsemane. In a Christlike act of empathy, you can too. It is my belief that if you have loved as I have loved, you would see there is no sin in my love. If you shared my gender experience, you would see there is no sin in my gender. If you could experience queerness with us, you would love us the way God loves us. It is my belief that as members of the Body of Christ, we may share the queer experience together. The body of Christ only functions when we unite in cohesiveness and embrace our differences.[27] Christ showed us that each of us has a unique experience that is worthy of consideration and empathy.

5. Spirit

In Mormonism, all knowledge is gained by the spirit of revelation, and those who seek diligently will have the mysteries of God shown to them.[28] As stated in 1 Nephi, "... the mysteries of God shall be unfolded unto them, by the power of the Holy Ghost, as well in these times as in times of old, and as well in times of old as in times to come; wherefore, the course of the Lord is one eternal round."[29] Joseph Smith also taught that "no man can receive the Holy Ghost without receiving revelations."[30] In the scriptures, we repeatedly read the Holy Spirit is how we gain knowledge and understanding.[31]

For me, the Spirit has been essential in helping me write this book. If it were not for my own experiences and personal witness of the divine nature of queerness, I would not be able to communicate these thoughts to you today. It is my hope that the Spirit be with me as I write and with you as you read. It is my hope that through continuing revelation, we may find spaces in our minds, hearts, and theology for queer folks. It is my hope that we do our best to hold these foundations of theology in balance as we seek further light and knowledge.

Theological responsibility

Changing policy must happen within the framework of our theology. For the queer community to be fully embraced by the Church, we are going to need a clear theological basis for any policy change or adaptation in ritual. I'm not suggesting a change to the fundamental principles in Mormon theology and doctrine, but rather advocate for a more robust vision of what Mormon theology and doctrine already includes.

Theology comes from somewhere. Theologies don't magically fall from the heavens into the laps of idle participants waiting to be told what to do. Theologies are developed from a network of participants. Past interpretations are precursors to new interpretations of theology. Mormon theology is especially primed for adaptation through continuing revelation.

Yet, some Latter-day Saints tend to believe that they didn't have a hand in interpreting or creating the theology they accept as true. There is a thick veil of historical amnesia which prevents participants from taking moral accountability for their imagined narrative. Our thoughts, words, and actions brought us to now, and it is harmful to assume our theology exists outside our agency and influence. When participants are sexist, the theology is sexist. When participants are racist, the theology is racist. When participants are heterosexist, the theology is heterosexist. When participants are cissexist, the theology is cissexist. As believing members of Mormon theology, we need to take responsibility for our influence in its development.

As free agents, we have the responsibility to seek further light and knowledge.[32] We are not meant to wait idly for commands, but to consciously seek after anything virtuous, lovely, of good report, or praiseworthy.[33] We are warned in Doctrine and Covenants, "For behold, it is not meet that I should command in all things; for he that is compelled in all things, the same is a slothful and not a wise servant; wherefore he receiveth no reward." Furthermore, we "should be anxiously engaged in a good cause, and do many things of their own free will, and bring to pass much righteousness."[34] As members of and participants in Mormonism, it is our duty to be anxiously engaged in good causes, including broadening our theological horizons to include all truths, including queer truths.

This is how we move into a state of theological maturity. We need to embrace our power as free agents to think and act as devout participants. This requires both humility and confidence. We need humility to recognize what we don't know, and confidence to seek further light and knowledge. Theological maturity means we can deconstruct and reconstruct theological perceptions with nuance and creativity. It means recognizing there are many theological interpretations, and we should not privilege dogmatic, harmful, or discursive elements. Theological maturity means we understand that differences, disagreements, and diversity are not to be feared, but understood. Theological maturity means taking responsibility for how our narratives and beliefs mold reality.

Speculative Theology

Speculative theology is like fanfiction. I mean that with respect, admiration, and reverence. Fanfiction comes from people who loved a story so much they didn't want it to end. They kept the story going even after its initial introduction.

Fanfiction is a form of fan labor. With fan labor, we bring stories to life. We create music, art, activities, conferences, study groups, and even costumes to make our stories real. Fanfictionalists invest significant time and resources into their work without the promise of monetary compensation. Bringing our most beloved stories to life is what fans do. It's also worth noting that fanfiction is created by the masses and rarely by the original author. Fanfiction is a communal exchange among the people. Sometimes people will question whether or not the fanfictionalist is staying true to the author's original intention—which is of deep importance to the fans. Fanfiction must be relatable to the story's original canon to be embraced by other fans.

Speculative theology functions similarly. To pontificate on the meanings and possibilities of theology is a form of worship and labor. It means that I love this story so much I want it to live, not just in my head but among the hearts of adherents everywhere who share my passion for Mormon theology. We, adherents of Mormon theology, create music, art, activities, conferences, study groups, and even costumes to bring our stories to life in temples, homes, conference centers, and churches around the world. Speculative theology is not disrespectful to theology. It is perhaps one of the highest compliments a devout adherent can give the original author. Surely worshipers will and should debate the merits of various speculative theologies. It's part of the process of common consent.[35]

Theology, especially speculative theology, is a communal endeavor. Theological development is strangely one of the most democratic aspects of Mormonism. Together, let us inquire into the queerness of Mormon theology and use our common love of Mormonism as a guide. Collectively, we have the power to manifest our sincerest beliefs through both faith and works.[36]

CHAPTER 2

Concerning God

In my youth, I was told that I was made in the image of God, that I am of divine nature, and that all are alike unto God.[1] These sentiments found in scripture are part of a doctrine that Mormons cherish. As a child, I felt powerful knowing there was godly potential in my being every time I sang "I am a Child of God." What an empowering idea it is to be made in the image of God and to eventually inherit God's glory.[2] Humanity holds the seeds of divinity.

In my adult life, these ideas have developed beyond elementary interpretations. If we want to take the scriptures seriously, we have to decide what it means to be made in the image of God. What image of God have we created through our art, music, pronouns, rituals, and worship? If all are made in the image of God, what exactly is God's image? Does God look like me? Does God look like you? If we are both made in the image of God, which of us more resembles the image of God? Does God have skin that is both black and white? Does God have a masculine or feminine body? What do our representations of the image of God say about us? As I have pondered these questions, I have become increasingly convinced that God is far more than I imagined in my youth.

God is Immanent

According to Mormon theology, God is immanent—which means that God exists within a material world. We can also think of this as a divine presence among and within us. All material creation is filled with immanence, even if we cannot see or recognize it. According to Mormon scripture, "There is no such thing as immaterial matter. All spirit is matter, but it is more fine or pure, and can only be discerned by pure eyes."[3] Furthermore, the term "light of Christ" is often used to describe the immanence of God that "fills the immensity of space."[4] The "light of Christ" is the presence of God that gives all things life. It is the "light of Christ" which connects us with God's immanence as we become one with God.[5]

Not only is God immanent, but we are also taught to love our fellow beings as we love God. If you have done it unto one of the least of God's children, you have done it unto God.[6] There is no clear distinction between us and God when we are coeternal with God; our intelligence is intimately and inextricably bound with God's intelligence.[7] Even before we were flesh, we were intelligences with God.[8] When we do unto each other, we do unto God. When we do unto animals, we do unto God. When we do unto our planet, we do unto God. Life is God's eternal intelligence.

Accepting the full immanence of God means looking outside of ourselves to see what is separate from us is actually within us. If we are all immanent with God, then we are part of the other, and the other is part of us. I do not intend this to be a secular humanist interpretation of scripture where humanism replaces God. This means that God is within and surrounds us. In Mormonism, we are coeternal with God.[9]

God is Singular and Plural

God is singular in oneness, wholeness, and immanence with humanity, but this oneness is simultaneously dependent on plurality. God is both singular and plural. This idea can be seen in the scriptures when God is referred to as *us*.[10] Similarly, the scriptures state, "Ye are gods; and all of you are children of the most High."[11] And the Doctrine & Covenants speaks of a time "in the which nothing shall be withheld, whether there be one God or many gods, they shall be manifest."[12]

God also exists in plurality in a Council of Gods.[13] This is noted in Joseph Smith's King Follett Sermon, an essential discourse explaining our relationship with God. In the sermon, Joseph Smith expands on the idea of multiple Gods. "In the beginning the head of Gods called a council of the Gods. They came together and concocted a plan to create the world and people it. When we begin to learn this way, we begin to learn the only true God, and what kind of being we have got to worship."[14] Here, we can see that God exists with other divine beings that Joseph called gods. In the beginning, there was more than just one god, but a plurality of gods who counseled together as the true God.

While many see Mormonism as a monotheistic religion that worships a deity referred to as Heavenly Father with masculine pronouns, this is not a complete, nor robust, understanding of Mormon theology. Mormons are polytheists—meaning they believe and worship more than one material, anthropomorphized deity.[15] Mormonism rejects the traditional Triune God that most Christians believe in and asserts that God the Father, Jesus Christ, and the Holy Spirit are three separate beings—though the Holy Spirit has no body.[16] The Godhead consists of three distinct entities. Mormons who claim to worship only one God, God the Father, also implicitly worship God the Mother when it is their combined union that makes godhood possible. While worship rituals and intentions may vary among adherents, worshiping one God doesn't make sense when God cannot attain godhood alone. Worshiping only God the Father implies worship of His godhood which is dependent on God the Mother.

God the Father cannot be God without God the Mother. As Erastus Snow, a nineteenth-century Latter-day Saint apostle, avowed, "If I believe anything God has ever said about himself... I must believe that deity consists of man and woman."[17] It is only through the sealed union of both male and female that God attains godhood in Mormon theology.[18] We are the spirit children of Heavenly Parents—plural. The nature of God is such that the Godhead has no God unless it includes male and female representation. In Mormonism, worshiping God the Father without God the Mother is nonsensical, for He is not God without She, and She is not God without He. We are symbiotically created in the image of God, both male and female.[19] In this sense, God is diverse and includes the image of all genders in God's material plurality. God's materiality and embodiment, whether through one body or many, plural or singular, is queer encompassing. There may exist many Gods of various genders in the council of the Gods.

I would also like to make clear that I am not making an appeal to heteronormative assumptions about how spirit children are created and reared. Under the umbrella of "God" there are many possible parental formations and familial dynamics. The union of man and woman doesn't mandate cisnormative and heteronormative ideas concerning copulation, reproduction, or orientation. What Mormon theology does mandate is sealings, alliances, partnerships, and cooperation among diverse genders. There are many more projections of God beyond cisgender, heterosexual assumptions when all gender identities and anatomies are made in the image of God.

Even beyond a godhead containing three separate material beings, including a God composed of both female and male identities in a sealed union, the theology can be taken further. God is a community of plural beings. Each of us may act as a representative of God when we use priesthood power to act in God's name—which does not necessarily require ordination.[20] God lives and breathes with each of their children. Each of us is the material image of God. We are literally made in their likeness. God is a community intimately intertwined with the materiality of every living entity. God is life—wholly, singly, and plurally. The common and reductive androcentric, heteronormative projection of an all-encompassing God is an incomplete and harmful representation of God's plurality and fullness. In Mormonism, gods create gods in worlds without end, and no god exists independent of their community, heritage, or posterity. The community that is God reflects the image of all life, not just men or even humans. God is the material manifestation of eternal life, and that image resides in each of us.

God is Dynamic

All material is in motion. If God is material, as Mormonism supposes, then neither God, nor life, is in a static state. Eternal progression mandates a dynamic God who is learning and growing along with humanity. If we are coeternal intelligences with God, our growth is reflected in the Gods as they grow with us. We are God's eternal progression.

As a Mormon, I see evolution as something exciting and faith-affirming rather than as a principle antithetical to theism. In Mormonism, our aspirations are not simply to be like God, but to join God, live in their presence, and be gods ourselves.[21] For me, this is one of the most profoundly beautiful doctrines of Mormonism. God isn't this unknowable, immaterial, metaphysical, supernatural entity. God is a product of spiritual and physical evolution, just like you. God was once a human, like us, and we can become gods too. We believe that there are Gods who eternally evolve in worlds without end in a process of eternal progression. In this sense, the Mormon idea of God is both compatible with and dependent upon evolution. This God is not an "omni" God. Terms like omnipotence, omniscience, omnibenevolence cannot be applied in a strict sense to God; otherwise, there would be no eternal progression or eternal increase. Progression requires change. There is no such thing as static progression. It might be useful to think of God being an "omni" God in relation to our limited knowledge, power, and experience, but in a strict philosophical sense, the Mormon God cannot be an "omni" God and progress eternally.

In Mormonism, we do not aspire simply to be like God, but to join God, live in God's presence, and be gods ourselves—also called *theosis*. "God was once as we are now, and is exalted, and sits enthroned in yonder heavens! That is the great secret. Here, then, is eternal life—to know the only wise and true God; and you have got to learn how to be gods yourselves, the same as all gods have done before you."[22] Not only are we coeternal and immanent with God, but we also have the potential to enjoy the same privileges and powers that God does, as joint-heirs with Christ.[23] We and God are dynamic participants in *theosis*.

If God is eternally progressing, both God as a referent and God as a sense are changing. Our perceptions of the gods we worship are constantly changing. To a certain extent, what we perceive is all we know, so if we are to know more, we must adjust our perceptions. What I speculate about God today will change in the future, and that's how it should be. Our projections of God should evolve upon further light and knowledge.

God is Intelligence

In Doctrine and Covenants, we read, "The glory of God is intelligence, or, in other words, light and truth."[24] Furthermore, we are glorified by gaining intelligence and knowledge.[25] When Eve and Adam partook of the fruit of knowledge in the Garden of Eden, their eyes were opened, and they were made aware of their ignorance. God said, "Behold, the man is become as one of us, to know good and evil."[26] This scripture demonstrates the plurality of Gods and the notion that increased knowledge is essential to our godly progression. We gain knowledge gradually in an ongoing process. Line upon line, precept on precept.[27] The more knowledge we gain, the godlier we become.

Mormon scripture also supposes that whatever intelligence is gained here on earth will be brought forth in the resurrection. Moreover, if a person gains more knowledge and intelligence in this life, they will have an advantage in the world to come.[28] Gaining knowledge and intelligence requires that we act as free agents.[29] According to scripture, agency is necessary to advance in intelligence and ultimately achieve godhood—as demonstrated when Eve and Adam chose to partake of the fruit of knowledge.

Thus far, we can gather that God is a community of interconnected, progressing, super-intelligent, free agents. This is the goal we are to aspire to, worship, and emulate. However, intelligence alone is not enough to qualify for godliness. We must also increase in love, compassion, and charity.

God is Love

God loves because God is love. The scriptures say if we dwell in love, we dwell in God,[30] and if we do not know love, we do not know God.[31] I suspect it is only through radically loving each other that we will ever come to know God. I'm confident that if God is love, then to the extent that we oppress love, we oppress our godly potential. To become God is to dwell in love.

One example of love we ought to follow is exemplified by Jesus in a more robust Christology. Jesus said the greatest commandment was to love God and each other. All other commandments hinge on this commandment.[32] Jesus then invites each of us to join him in the body of Christ, also called *Christosis*.[33] As members of the body of Christ, this means each of us is anointed to do God's work as diverse agents. Disciples of Christ will be known by their ability to love one another.[34] There is no clear distinction between loving God, loving Jesus, loving Christ, and loving your fellow beings. If you have done it unto one of the least of God's children, you have done it unto God.[35] Anyone loving their fellow brothers, sisters, and siblings is loving God also.

As Christians and members of the body of Christ, love is our common purpose and our most important goal. But what does one body in Christ mean?[36] How do we find unity in diversity? Do we think it will happen without significant emotional labor, vulnerability, sacrifice, or bravery? The scriptures say to love your enemies and do good to them that hate you.[37] The scriptures say to love and pray for those that persecute you.[38] These are not casual requests. Atoning isn't easy. Reconciling isn't simple. Forgiveness isn't painless. Love isn't effortless. I do not expect this sentiment to be received easily, but as members of the body of Christ, it is imperative that we learn to love non-exclusively and unconditionally. We must be brave in confronting our insecurities and find the humanity and divinity within one another. We must do this not only when we find it easy to love, but also when we find it difficult to love. Gods are Gods because they learned to love another when loving wasn't easy.

As Latter-day Saints, we are also commanded to establish Zion on our path to godhood.[39] I imagine Zion as a community held together with love, not fear. There is no fear in love.[40] I'll admit, there are times

I still fear. I fear convention. I fear my religious community's apathy toward further revelation. I fear the unfulfilled potential of humanity. I fear that my community is only willing to aspire to Zion when it's convenient. Is Zion willing to include the queer and peculiar? I honestly don't know. The acceptance of the queer through unconditional love isn't entirely up to me. I need grace, just like you.[41]

God has promised not to override our agency and compel us to love and embrace each other. We must learn to love one another of our own volition the way God loves us. In other words, we must love queer folks the way God loves queer folks, and we must keep this in mind as we build Zion: God's hands are bound by our agency. God cannot reveal to us what we cannot accept.[42]

God's love is necessarily plural, especially when God is plural. There is more than enough to go around. If we are immanent with God in an intimately bound network of coeternal intelligences, God's love must be plural. God is no respecter of persons, and all are alike unto God.[43] The words "God so loved the world," cannot be read without its plural implications for all intelligences. I use the term "plural love" rather than "omnibenevolence" precisely because there is always room for greater development under the premise of eternal progression. God's love is great, our love is great, yet there is still room for greater love to be shared among each other and the Gods. In Mormon theology, love is a principle of plurality.

To become Gods, are we willing to be of the same mind, one toward another?[44] Zion was called Zion because the people were of one heart and one mind.[45] I don't know if I can think of anything more intimate than being of the same mind with one or many souls in an interconnected network of intelligence.

I know words like intimacy and plurality can be problematic when common vernacular often limits ideas of intimacy and plurality with sexual or romantic partners, but that's not my experience. Sexual expressions are only one modality of intimacy and love. To be sure, sharing my body with a lover is an intimate act, but I have also shared my body with my three children, and sexual arousal was not a motive or result. They lived inside me. I gave them life. I fed them at my breast. Even bodily intimacy cannot be limited to sexual desire. Intimacy comes from shared interpersonal moments that engender closeness—to be of one heart and one mind. This is what it means to have intimate relationships in the community we call "Zion." When I think of how Gods love one another, I imagine a love that may include sexual intimacy but far surpasses it.

People speak of love as if loving a person somehow takes away from the love you have for another, as if love were a zero-sum game. In such a model, love becomes a resource where its value lies in its scarcity, not in its unconditional abundance. If that is the case, love is prized in its exclusivity. Your loss is my gain. Your gain is my loss. It would be like saying that God's love is meaningless because They give to all Their children unconditionally instead of a prime few who "deserve it" or "earned it." This would be like suggesting that the Atonement is less valuable when it is universal. Is that really the myth we want to tell? I don't think I could call myself a theist if I believed that God's love is a finite resource to be squabbled over, or that Jesus's Atonement is less of a gift when he gives it to all.

Above all, God is loving, and we should be too. Charity is the pure love of Christ, and charity never fails. If it is our purpose to become gods, we must learn to love plurally as They do. Unity through plural love will be the lighthouse that will guide us safely toward celestial vistas.[46]

God is Liberating

While many may see obedience to God's commandments as limiting, I find the opposite to be true. Obedience to God's commandments is one of the most liberating aspects of Mormon theology. For me, it is not a matter of if we should be obedient, but rather how we should be obedient.

God gave us the greatest commandment through Jesus Christ. The greatest commandment is to love God and love each other. All other commandments hinge on this commandment. If any other command or request conflicts with the first commandment of "thou shalt love," it should be reworked, reimagined, or discarded. No other command can supersede God's ultimate commandment to love.

> Master, which is the great commandment in the law? Jesus said unto him, Thou shalt love the Lord thy God with all thy heart, and with all

thy soul, and with all thy mind. This is the first and great commandment. And the second is like unto it, Thou shalt love thy neighbour as thyself. On these two commandments hang all the law and the prophets.[47]

God didn't say, "ye must be obedient to unrighteous authoritarians, tyrants, priests, or patriarchs." God didn't say, "ye must be obedient to racist, sexist, heterosexist, or cissexist policies." God didn't say "ye must vote for a specific political party." God didn't say "women shall not seek after priesthood ordination." God didn't say "ye must take all commands unquestionably, ye shall not doubt religious leaders, or ye shall obey all requests without thinking." God didn't say "when the prophet speaks the thinking is done." No. God didn't say any of these things in our scriptures.

According to Mormon theology, God said love Us and love your neighbor. No other commandment, rule, policy, or request may conflict with the first. Jesus said this was not to destroy the existing law but to fulfill the law.[48] The other laws matter, but love is the commandment that all other laws hinge upon. This is explicit permission to disobey a teaching that conflicts with God's greatest commandment: to love.

Any leader who is telling you to obey a command that conflicts with loving God and your neighbor is acting as a false prophet. Keep in mind that the founder of Mormonism, Joseph Smith, Jr., taught that a prophet is only a prophet when acting as such.[49] False teachings often happen with the best of intentions but with harmful consequences. False teachings include the idea that queer relationships are "counterfeit" or incapable of godly love.[50] False teachings may even include trying to convince you that a policy excluding children from baptism is made from their so-called love.[51] However, if their so-called love doesn't promote love, joy, and life, then it is not love.[52] If their so-called love promotes depression, anxiety, hopelessness, and thoughts and feelings of suicide among queer Mormons, then it is not love.[53] That's not how love works. Love should not make queer Mormons want to die. Harmful requests, mandates, and policies made under the disguise of love should be resisted through strict obedience to God's first commandment.

Armed with godly agency, we must discover better ways of loving one another. We are commanded to do so.[54] Half of love is how it is given, but the other half is how it is received. An abuser could punch a victim in the face and say they are doing it out of their so-called love, but if the victim does not receive the punch as an expression of love the punch cannot be deemed an act of love—even if love was the intention. How the punch was received matters. If a leader is telling you it is an act of love to exclude same-sex couples from the temple, ask the same-sex couple if they feel loved by that policy of exclusion. If you are ever in doubt about whether or not a request, policy, commandment, talk, or even comment is an act of love, ask the person(s) whom the policy, talk, or comment affects.

We only know and prophesy in part, but charity never fails.[55] Quite literally, with God, love wins. Love wins even when policies and teachings fall short. Together, we need to find out how to best love the queer members of our community, and that starts by listening to how queer Saints received said expressions of love. As Elder Ballard said, "We need to listen to and understand what our LGBT brothers and sisters are feeling and experiencing."[56]

Obedience fundamentally requires agency. To obey meaningfully, we must think and act as free agents. God will not micromanage our obedience to Their commandment to love God and each other. "For behold, it is not meet that I should command in all things; for he that is compelled in all things, the same is a slothful and not a wise servant; wherefore he receiveth no reward."[57] Furthermore, we "should be anxiously engaged in a good cause, and do many things of their own free will, and bring to pass much righteousness."[58] Obedience to God's greatest command is not simple, dogmatic, or easy. It requires our thoughtful engagement as free agents. At times you must disobey an unrighteous authority to obey a higher authority, and that higher authority is love. God is not interested in robotic obedience, or we wouldn't have a need for agency—that was Satan's plan. Each member of the body of Christ has the duty and responsibility to obey God's commandments according to the dictates of their conscience with an open heart and willing mind.[59]

In this context, obedience to God's greatest commandment can liberate us from dogma, tyranny, apathy, superstition, and thoughtlessness. If the greatest commandment is to love, by all means, be obedient. Obey God with every fiber of your being. God is love.[60] Feel love in your bones—let it motivate our every thought, decision, and action as we strive toward our divine potential.

God is Purposeful

God desires us to become just like Them.[61] This makes us Gods in embryo with the potential to have all the divine attributes which God has—that we might become exalted, embodied, super-intelligent, immortal beings just like Them. Essentially, God intends for us to be happy, benevolent, immortal beings.

Happiness is essential to God's purpose. We are that we might have joy.[62] Joseph Smith observed, "Happiness is the object and design of our existence; and will be the end thereof, if we pursue the path that leads to it; and this path is virtue, uprightness, faithfulness, holiness, and keeping all the commandments of God."[63] In the Book of Mormon, God's plan is called "The Great Plan of Happiness."[64] God's plan is to increase the love, life, joy, and happiness in the universe—even for queer folks. If our policies, culture, speculative theologies, or dogmas have deviated from love, life, joy, happiness, and flourishing, we need to correct our mistakes to better exemplify God's "Plan of Happiness" for all God's children.

In the book of Moses, we are taught that God's work and glory is to bring to pass the immortality and eternal life of Their children.[65] God's goals are our goals. We too should be working toward the progression of happiness, love, immortality, life, and increase of intelligence. However, we are not simply meant to be immortal like God, but God desires us to become Gods too.[66] Whether we call it becoming like God, becoming Gods, or knowing God, this is the promise of eternal life if we choose to grow into godly beings.[67] There is room for all of us to share in God's glory through the process of *theosis*.[68]

The most explicity account of Joseph Smith teaching the doctrine of *theosis* is found in the King Follet Sermon. He taught we are endowed with divine powers. We hail from a divine nature. We are gods in the making if we choose to grow into such. Joseph Smith taught that God was once as we are now and is exalted. "That is the great secret. Here, then, is eternal life—to know the only wise and true God; and you have got to learn how to be gods yourselves, the same as all gods have done before you."[69] Not only are we coeternal and immanent with God, we also have the potential to enjoy the same privileges and powers God does, as joint-heirs with Christ.[70] Just imagine, in the taxonomy of the Gods, the difference between the Gods and us is not a matter of kind, but degree.

This doctrine boldly taught by Joseph Smith was also taught by other early Mormon leaders, including early Mormon women. When I look back at the early Mormon women, I am inspired by their dedication to the doctrine of *theosis*. Early Mormon women embodied the notion that godhood includes more than one gender. Below are three of my favorite passages from *At the Pulpit: 185 Years of Discourse by Latter-day Saint Women*, demonstrating that *theosis* is an endeavor that reaches beyond androcentric gender norms.

> We have been instructed that each one of us in our organizations is endowed with the germs of every faculty requisite to constitute a god or goddess. These little ones in their mother's arms have the germs of all the capacity which we exhibit, and what constitutes the difference between them and ourselves? Merely a lack of development in them, and this development requires cultivation, energy, and perseverance. The organization of the Female Relief Society places the sisters in positions to bring into exercise and thus develop all of our faculties: that's in doing good to others, we benefit ourselves . . . let us try to realize our responsibilities and honor our position. (Eliza R. Snow)[71]

> Why is it today there is so much broader a view taken of woman's position than before? Because woman herself is beginning to feel that she is an enlightened, responsible being, with a mind capable of the highest intelligence, with talents that it is her duty to develop and use for the advancement and elevation of the human family. This feeling is gradually but steadily growing; it is being felt throughout the world and it will continue to grow until it becomes a power in the earth. (Martha "Mattie" Horne Tingey)[72]

> It is proper on occasions like this to consider such topics as shall be of the highest benefit to womankind; into my mind, it is fitting to discuss here that capacity of mind in which woman is preeminently fitted to excel [. . .] They that knock with study and faith's assurance have the narrow way opened to them and I received into communion with the infinite Father and Mother, are permitted to enter hollowed mansions, to attend the school of the profits, and by advancing

> steps, to reach the school of the gods, where they learn the process by which worlds are organized by the combining of eternal, intelligent, obedient elements; The uses for which worlds are called into existence; the manner in which they are controlled; and the laws of progression by which all begins and animate things are perfected and glorified in their respective spheres. (Sarah M. Kimball)[73]

These were bold words for their time. The idea of men becoming gods was a radical idea, but the idea of women becoming gods was even more radical. These women demonstrate that *theosis* was a larger endeavor than male singletons reaching for divinity in their hubris. These women demonstrated that a person's gender isn't basis to exclude them from *theosis*, the school of prophets, and the school of the gods.

From then to now, the doctrine of *theosis* is still taught within Mormon theology. We can see it in our temples, worship, and rituals. Elder D. Todd Christofferson taught we are predestined to receive all that God has in store for us.[74] Elder Dallin H. Oaks taught that "our theology begins with heavenly parents. Our highest aspiration is to be like them."[75] Elder Gordon B. Hinckley bore his testimony that God's work is to bring to pass the eternal life of all generations.[76] Elder Boyd K. Packer taught that we are the same species as God, and godhood is our destiny.[77]

Finally, I love the way Elder Jeffery R. Holland unapologetically teaches the doctrine of *theosis* while speaking at a devotional in Tempe, Arizona. Not only does he affirm one of Mormonism's most unique and empowering doctrines, but he also affirms that we are active participants in this work.

> We're the church that says we're gods and goddesses in embryo. We're the Church that says we're kings and queens. We're priests and priestesses. People accuse us of heresy. They say we're absolutely heretical, non-Christians because we happen to believe what all the prophets taught and that is that we are children of God, joint-heirs with Christ. We just happen to take the scriptures literally that kids grow up to be like their parents. But how does that happen? How does godliness happen? Do we just pop up? Are we just going to pop up out of the grave? Hallelujah, it's resurrection morning! Give me a universe or two. Bring me some worlds to run! I don't think so. That doesn't sound like line upon line or precept upon precept to me. How do you become godly? You do godly things. That's how you become godly. And you practice, and you practice, and you practice.[78]

Theosis is not a fad doctrine. Our theology cannot be properly understood without the widespread implications of what *theosis* is and what it means for all people to become godly. In Mormon theology, godhood is the goal not just for men but all of us.

This means God is far more diverse than a single, divine, omnipotent male who never changes, progresses, or increases. God is reflected in the face and spirit of every living intelligence who has ever lived. God is the hope that we may overcome the limitations which left us to die. God is what we may become in capacities we have only begun to discover by embracing a more robust theism to enhance our understanding of the evolutionary process of eternal progression. God is eternal life, and that image resides in all God's children, including the queer and peculiar.

God is Respectful

God respects agency and work. Mormon theology puts heavy emphasis on human agency and on God's promise not to interfere in human agency. Mormonism teaches that it was Satan who, in the pre-existence, wanted to "destroy the agency of man."[79] In Mormonism we are free to choose our own future—even if that means our own destruction.[80] God will not impinge on our agency to create our own future. God grants us blessings according to our desires.[81] If we want celestial glory, it will be of our own choosing.[82] We have a choice in our future, and our future will be according to our desires, faith, works, and grace.

Mormons have always been a people who value work. We are a people of "doing." We take the scriptures seriously and affirm faith without works is dead.[83] In Doctrine and Covenants, we read, "For I, the Lord, will judge all men according to their works, according to the desire of their hearts."[84] If we do not work, we cannot be saved. If we want to become gods, we need to put forth an effort. Both agency and work are necessary.

The world is changing. Humanity is evolving. The question is, how do we want to evolve? God isn't going to stop us. It may seem like no one is behind the wheel when everyone is behind the wheel, but that is not an excuse to avoid introspectively asking yourself, what kind of god do you want to be? Will we worship and become gods who reign in tyranny over others without regard for their agency or desires?[85] Will we marginalize outliers without considering their plight? Will we oppress queerness and call it "sin" or open our hearts and minds to continuing revelation? Or will we follow the example of Jesus? Will we become one in Christ, even queer in Christ, by unifying ourselves in all our diversity?[86] Will we genuinely embrace the doctrine of inclusion?[87] Will we embrace our power as children of gods?

Celestial glory is right here if we choose it and prepare for it.[88] Doctrine and Covenants prophecies the earth "may be prepared for the celestial glory . . . that bodies who are of the celestial kingdom may possess it forever and ever."[89] Celestial glory is prophesied to be right here, on earth, if we choose to cultivate such a godly community for all bodies. God has a purpose—that we should become gods—and it is up to us to fulfill that purpose when God respects our agency.

CHAPTER 3

Concerning Christ

Jesus Christ is of utmost importance in Mormon theology. The Prophet Joseph Smith stated that all "things which pertain to our religion are only appendages" to the Atonement of Christ.[1] Jesus is the chief exemplar of how we are to become gods. As siblings with Jesus and offspring of God, we are "then heirs; heirs of God, and joint-heirs with Christ," if we join Jesus as members of the body of Christ.[2] This is how we will be glorified together with Jesus. He is the example we must follow on our path to godhood. In Mormonism, there is no other way to be saved but through Christ.

Jesus as Queer

In Gethsemane, Jesus didn't simply suffer for the sins of men; he also suffered "the pains of every living creature, both men, women, and children, who belong to the family of Adam."[3] To repeat, he suffered for every "living creature." Furthermore, "He that ascended up on high, as also he descended below all things, in that he comprehended all things, that he might be in all and through all things, the light of truth."[4] In Gethsemane, Jesus wasn't simply atoning for men's sins, women's sins, queer sins, or even humanity's sins. He ascended above and descended below all things so that he might "comprehend all things." Jesus suffered every pain, sickness, infirmity, sorrow, disparity, injustice, and oppression imaginable. He knew the entirety of human experience. I cannot imagine anyone having a queerer experience than what Jesus had in Gethsemane.

Imagine with me, the Garden of Gethsemane, among the olive trees that Jesus' consciousness was linked, intertwined, connected, or merged with every person who ever lived or ever would live in the world. He didn't know our experiences by analogy; he actually experienced them so he could comprehend all things. He experienced it all. It's no wonder he sweat blood.[5] What type of body could withstand the suffering of all humanity, gendered or otherwise?

In Gethsemane, Jesus experienced the pains of a person dying of cancer. He experienced what it is like to be a queer kid who is constantly bullied. He experienced the birthing pains of every mother who ever lived or would live. He experienced the embarrassment of a gay boy having an erection at the sight of his school crush in the locker room. He experienced conversion therapy. He experienced rejection. He experienced the brutal physical and psychological attacks that trans women endure. He experienced the acid poured on a women's face for her defiance to the patriarchs. He experienced the fear, grief, and sorrow of every parent who has buried their child. He experienced sex slavery. He experienced his first period. He experienced menstruation, not simply from a vagina but from every pore of his body. He experienced rape. He experienced catcalls. He experienced hunger. He experienced disease. He experienced an ectopic pregnancy. He experienced an abortion. He experienced a miscarriage and stillbirth. He experienced the Holocaust. He experienced war—both the killing and being killed. He experienced internment camps. He experienced depression, anxiety, and suicide. He experienced sleeping on the street with the homeless. He experienced the slave master's whip on his back and the noose around his neck. He knew the fear of every black mother who kissed her son before he left the house, praying he would return home safely. He experienced the effects of unrighteous dominion, corrupt politicians, and all manner of injustice. He experienced the migrant mother with no food or diapers for her baby as she desperately walked north in search of a better life. He experienced having his child taken away from him at the border due to "legal complications." He experienced it all—every death, every cut, every tear, every pain, every sorrow, every bit of suffering imaginable and beyond human imagination. He experienced an onslaught of suffering, which was so great that it took a god to bear it. He experienced death and came through the other side to show us the way.

When we account for the full robustness of Jesus' experience in Gethsemane, the pronoun "He" doesn't seem adequate. Nor would "She." A being who has known through personal experience all the world's suffering, gendered or otherwise, becomes "They." Jesus Christ entered Gethsemane as "He" but left as "They." Jesus tapped into the consciousness of the entire world, and that's not an experience that can be dismissed as non-queer.

I am not suggesting that his literal sexual orientation, gender identity, or preferred pronouns changed in any sort of simplistic sense. I am suggesting that, by sharing a consciousness with every gender, race, orientation, and ability, Jesus became exceptionally aware of the pains of the world. He consciously became both male and female, cisgender and transgender, agender and pangender, black and white, strong and weak, heterosexual and homosexual. I am suggesting Jesus the Christ left Gethsemane queer. The Atonement was a queer experience.

After Gethsemane, the now-queer Jesus was taken to Pontius Pilate. Jesus was accused of "perverting the nation."[6] Pilot searched, looking for a reason to justify killing Jesus, but finally said, "I find in him no fault at all."[7] Even so, Jesus was scourged, and they put a crown of thorns on his head before beating him.[8] Again, Pilot said to the masses, "I find no fault in him,"[9] but the crowds persisted and called out for Jesus' crucifixion.[10] Even the customary pardon of Passover did not spare Jesus. Barabbas, a notorious prisoner,[11] was pardoned instead. When Pilate saw that the crowds would not stop until they saw Jesus dead, he washed his hands before the masses and said, "I am innocent of the blood of this just person: see ye to it."[12] Jesus was then taken to Calvary and crucified.[13]

As I read the story of the crucifixion in my youth, the character I fixated on the most was Pilate. I felt both anger and compassion toward Pilate. He had political power. He could have saved Jesus! Yet, he didn't.

The pressure of the masses was too great. To be fair to Pilate, he repeatedly tried to secure the safe release of Jesus before giving in. However, even though Pilate did not commit the greater sin, he still ought to be held accountable for his part in Jesus' death. Sorry, Pilate, you don't get to wash your hands of accountability.[14]

While I have compassion for Pilate, we cannot allow ourselves to become the Pilate in our own narrative. Queer abuse, assault, murder, and suicide are realities. Queer Latter-day Saints are suffering, even dying, and instead of listening to queer survivors, we debate the statistics and manipulate numbers to displace our communal responsibility to care for the least among us. Too many have attempted to wash their hands of accountability.

This does not mean that there is a single solution to prevent queer suicide, or that we can prevent someone from taking their life if that's what they decide to do. However, queer suicide among Latter-day Saints is a reality, and we all play a role in it when we cultivate an environment that rejects queer identities and relationships. Through our action, and inaction, we are sending a clear message to queer Latter-day Saints, "You don't belong here."

What have we done to save the innocent? Pilate tried. He tried multiple times, but when the pressure was too great, he washed his hands as an innocent queer Jesus was put to death. We have blood on our hands, and we cannot claim our innocence in the narrative when queer people across the globe are dying.

We, as members of the body of Christ, must join together to make Christ's atonement meaningful for every member of the body. Pilate relinquished his accountability, while Jesus embraced it. Jesus didn't say, "I wash my hands of your sins. Your fate will be decided by the fearmongering of angry mobs. I tried. You're on your own." No, Jesus said, "I will give my flesh for the life of the world."[15] He said, "My blood is shed for many for the remission of sins."[16] His blood was spilled to cleanse us all of sin.[17] He offered up an infinite atonement.[18] He didn't just take responsibility for himself. He took on the infinite responsibility of all of us. As disciples of Christ, we must do the same.

The Body of Christ

Jesus Christ's atonement, when understood comprehensively, is not limited to Jesus, but potentially includes all of humanity. In the scriptures, we are taught that we are all the body of Christ.

> For as the body is one, and hath many members, and all the members of that one body, being many, and one body: so also is Christ. For the body is not one member, but many. And whether one member suffer, all the members suffer with it; or one member be honoured, all the members rejoice with it. Now ye are the body of Christ and members in particular.[19]

Christ is explicitly telling us that Christ extends beyond Jesus. Christ includes us. These scriptures remind me of David Basden's rendition of *Christ Has No Body Now on Earth But Yours*.[20] The lyrics are as follows:

> Christ has no body but yours;
> No hands, no feet, on earth but yours.
> Yours are the eyes through which He looks with compassion on this world;
> Yours are the feet with which He walks to do good;
> Yours are the hands with which He blesses all the world.
> Yours are the hands, Yours and the feet;
> Yours are the eyes; You are His body.
> Christ has no body now but yours;
> No hands, no feet on earth but yours.
> Yours are the eyes through which He looks with compassion on this world;
> Christ has no body now on earth but yours.
> Amen.

As members of the body of Christ, we can suffer with humanity. We can weep with humanity. We can rejoice with humanity. We can reconcile with humanity. We can atone with humanity. This is what it means to become the body of Christ—to join Jesus in atoning. Our doctrine mandates our participation. We must take on the shape of one another's pain in Christ.

Diversity in Christ

The word Christ comes from the Greek word *christos*, which means "anointed" or "anointed one." More specifically, this means to be anointed with oil because God has chosen you to accomplish Their work. According to the biblical text, Jesus was chosen, anointed by God to be the exemplar and Savior of the world.

However, Jesus also invited each of us to join him as members of the body of Christ.[21] As members of the body of Christ, we are God's hands, feet, legs, eyes, heart, lungs, mind, and body. The body of Christ is explicitly diverse. Without diversity, the body's functionality would be lost.[22]

Imagine your own body as a metaphor for the body of Christ. Your body is composed of many different types of cells. Though your cells have different functions, they work in unison to achieve a specific goal—to keep you alive. Now, imagine your body without skin cells to protect your internal anatomy. Or imagine your body composed only of liver cells. Consider a body with no bone cells. The functionality of the human body depends on its diverse parts cohesively working together. We all depend on diversity.

In the body of Christ, each part is a valued member. The body of Christ is described as being one with every member, even the members perceived as being feeble, as necessary.[23] God is no respecter of persons, and all are alike unto God.[24] God did not say that we all need to have the same sexual orientation, that we need to identify with our gender assignment, that we need to have the same skin color, or that we need to belong to the same religious denomination to be a valued member of the body of Christ. No. God said each diverse member is a valued member, and we need to love each other.

The scriptures also say "that there should be no schisms" in the body of Christ.[25] Some have taken the concept of "no schisms" to mean there should be no difference—that we should all homogenize into sameness: the same likings, the same preferences, the same labels, the same functions, the same traditions, the same sexual orientation, even the same religion. Yet, that is the exact opposite of how the body of Christ operates. So, what does it mean to have "no schisms" in the body of Christ?

The answer is in the same verse as the warning. The scriptures tell us "no schisms" means "that the members should have the same care one for another." In other words, you don't get to kick someone out of the body of Christ for being different than you. It warns us that we should not be apathetic to the needs of other members. "No schisms" is not the condemnation of difference. "No schisms" is the condemnation of indifference. "No schisms" means we must care for one another while respecting our differences. It means when one member suffers, we all suffer. It means to weep with those who weep and rejoice with those who rejoice.[26] At times it seems impossible to live in such a godly paradox of constant weeping and rejoicing, but this is the unifying aim. Put simply, "no schisms" in the body of Christ means to love one another as yourself.[27]

I like the way President Uchtdorf highlights the importance of diversity within the Church is his General Conference talk, "Four Titles." Our diversity is an important part of how many parts create a greater whole.

> But while the Atonement is meant to help us all become more like Christ, it is not meant to make us all the same. Sometimes we confuse differences in personality with sin. We can even make the mistake of thinking that because someone is different from us, it must mean they are not pleasing to God. This line of thinking leads some to believe that the Church wants to create every member from a single mold—that each one should look, feel, think, and behave like every other. This would contradict the genius of God, who created every man different from his brother, every son different from his father. Even identical twins are not identical in their personalities and spiritual identities.
>
> It also contradicts the intent and purpose of the Church of Jesus Christ, which acknowledges and protects the moral agency—with all its far-reaching consequences—of each and every one of God's children. As disciples of Jesus Christ, we are united in our testimony of the restored gospel and our commitment to keep God's commandments. But we are diverse in our cultural, social, and political preferences.
>
> The Church thrives when we take advantage of this diversity and encourage each other to develop and use our talents to lift and strengthen our fellow disciples.[28]

When Jesus invited us to join him in the body of Christ, we are not only disciples in thought but also in deed. Faith without works is dead.[29] As members of the body of Christ each of us is anointed to do God's work, which is to follow the example of Jesus. And what did Jesus tell us to do? Jesus told us the greatest commandment was to love God and love your neighbor.

Queer in Christ

Together, we are becoming Christ. Mormon theology demands our participation in this endeavor. But how do we do that? How are we to become Christ? It is even possible to endure all that Jesus endured? Alone, we will fail, but together there is a chance we might succeed.

We take the sacrament every Sunday to remind us we are the body of Christ. "While they were eating, Jesus took bread, gave thanks and broke it, and gave it to his disciples, saying, 'Take it: this is my body.'"[30] We symbiotically take on the name of Christ each week in a religious ritual. We take the sacrament as a reminder to following Jesus' example.[31] We promise to take on Jesus's queer experience in Gethsemane every Sunday as members of the body of Christ. We promise to atone together. When we take the sacrament, we are made queer in Christ.

Becoming queer in Christ does not mean you have to change your pronouns, sexual orientation, identity labels, or gender performance. Becoming queer in Christ means that we encompass a broad spectrum of genders, orientations, races, abilities, and experiences. Embracing our collective queerness and peculiarity is an important step towards godhood because there is no other way to be saved, except by Christ.

I previously mentioned the diverse traumas that Jesus experienced while in Gethsemane. I want you to read the paragraph again. However, instead of reading the paragraph as "He experienced," I want you to read it as "We experienced." I want you to take on the name of Christ. The body of Christ is not "He," "She," or even "They." Christ is a "We." If we genuinely believe in taking on the name of Christ with Jesus, let's immersively consider what that might be like.

In Gethsemane, we experienced the pains of a person dying of cancer. We experienced what it is like to be a queer kid who is constantly bullied. We experienced the birthing pains of every mother who ever lived or would live. We experienced the embarrassment of a gay boy having an erection at the sight of his school crush in the locker room. We experienced conversion therapy. We experienced rejection. We experienced the brutal physical and psychological attacks that trans women endure. We experienced the acid poured on a woman's face for her defiance to the patriarchs. We experienced the fear, grief, and sorrow of every parent who has buried their child. We experienced sex slavery. We experienced our first period. We experienced menstruation, not simply from a vagina, but from every pore of our body. We experienced rape. We experienced catcalls. We experienced hunger. We experienced disease. We experienced an ectopic pregnancy. We experienced an abortion. We experienced a miscarriage and stillbirth. We experienced the Holocaust. We experienced war—both the killing and being killed. We experienced internment camps. We experienced depression, anxiety, and suicide. We experienced sleeping on the street with the homeless. We experienced the slave master's whip on our back and the noose around our neck. We knew the fear of every black mother who kissed her son before he left the house, praying he would return home safely. We experienced the effects of unrighteous dominion, corrupt politicians, and all manner of injustice. We experienced the migrant mother with no food or diapers for her baby as she desperately walked north in search of a better life. We experienced having our child taken away at the border due to "legal complications." We experienced it all—every death, every cut, every tear, every pain, every sorrow, every bit of suffering imaginable and beyond human imagination. We experienced an onslaught of suffering that was so great that it took a God to bear it. We experienced death and came through the other side to show each other the way.

 We must become that God. We must take on the pains of the world with one another in a collective act of charity. If this seems like an insurmountable goal, I would not blame you for uttering the words, "If it be possible, let this cup pass from me."[32] Even Jesus, the begotten son of Heavenly Parents, was sorrowful unto death.[33]

 This is what it means to take on the role of Christ. This is how to become gods. We must be brave enough to take on the pains of the world and reconcile every wrong. We must bear one another's burdens. We must take on the queerness of the atonement and reconcile in love, compassion, and charity. Charity is the pure love of Christ.[34] It will not fail us. We must emulate Jesus until we become Christ.[35] Keep in mind emulating Jesus is more than suffering; it is also atoning. Suffering for the sake of suffering will get us nowhere. We must take the necessary steps in transforming our suffering into motivation for reconciliation. That is how we take on the name of Christ.

Redemption

Matthew Wayne Shepard was a 21-year-old gay student at the University of Wyoming who was beaten, tortured, and left to die near Laramie on the night of October 6, 1998.[36] During the night of the attack, he was driven to a remote, rural location where he was robbed, pistol-whipped, and tortured. Two of his peers tied him to a fence, set him on fire, and left him to die in near-freezing temperatures. Reports said Shepard was so brutally beaten that his face was covered in blood, except where it had been partially cleansed by his tears.[37] Shepard was later found by a cyclist who mistook him for a scarecrow.[38] Shepard, in a coma, never regained consciousness and remained on full life support until he died six days after the attack. At Shepard's funeral, religious hate-mongers picketed with homophobic signs while chanting, "Fags die, God laughs." [39]

Is there any redemption for the trauma of this experience? What can be done to prevent the spilling of queer blood, whether by a hate crime or suicide? Is there any way to reconcile what has happened to Shepard? Is there any way to reconcile what has happened to queer bodies across the globe?

In *The Queer Bible Commentary*, Thomas Bohache states that we need not let Shepard's death be in vain. The horror and brutality of Shepard's death brought the issue of violence against queer bodies to public awareness.[40] Even after his death, Shepard's story was told. Like Jesus, his story lived on because his disciples shared his story. As stated in Terrance McNally's play *Corpus Christi*, "Jesus Christ did not die in vain because His disciples lived to spread His story. It is this generation's duty to make certain Matthew Shepard did not die in vain either." [41]

Sharing stories, awareness, and advocacy are important parts of redemption. Changing ourselves to be more benevolent is another important part of redemption. However, Mormon theology takes the idea of redemption even further. According to doctrine, we believe in the redemption of all things. So much that through Jesus Christ, Matthew Shepard might be wholly redeemed.

Latter-day Saints consider the resurrection of Jesus to be one of the most glorious events of all time. By being resurrected, He broke the bonds of death. Death would have no more dominion over Christ, including us.[42] It is in Christ that we all shall live again.[43] Not only that, but all will also be restored, including the brokenness of Matthew Shepard's body. The Book of Mormon states, "The soul shall be restored to the body, and the body to the soul; yea, and every limb and joint shall be restored to its body; yea, even a hair of the head shall not be lost; but all things shall be restored to their proper and perfect frame."[44]

As members of the body of Christ, redeeming our dead is also our responsibility. As disciples of Jesus, we commit to live as Jesus lived and do what Jesus would do. If Jesus broke the bonds of death, we must do that too, or at least invest all of our effort into trying. In the scriptures we read:

> So when this corruptible shall have put on incorruption, and this mortal shall have put on immortality, then shall be brought to pass the saying that is written, Death is swallowed up in victory. O death, where is thy sting? O grave, where is thy victory? The sting of death is sin; and the strength of sin is the law. But thanks be to God, which giveth us the victory through our Lord Jesus Christ. Therefore, my beloved brethren, be ye steadfast, unmoveable, always abounding in the work of the Lord, forasmuch as ye know that your labour is not in vain in the Lord.[45]

Note the final verse states we should be steadfast and always abounding in the work of the Lord. God's work is our work, and God's work is to bring to pass the immortality and eternal life of all of us.[46] Redeeming the dead means exactly what it says: we must redeem our dead. This is more than a metaphorical proposition. Jesus himself told us to raise the dead, "And as ye go, preach, saying, The kingdom of heaven is at hand. Heal the sick, cleanse the lepers, raise the dead, cast out devils: freely ye have received, freely give."[47] Jesus offered us this challenge, "Verily, verily, I say unto you, He that believeth on me, the works that I do shall he do also."[48] If we genuinely believe Jesus, we must become Christ and bring our prophecies to life.

Jesus Christ, the Redeemer and Savior of the world, set the example for us. When he raised Lazarus from the dead, he wasn't just metaphorically telling Lazarus's story and cherishing his memory. Lazarus wasn't just in a coma or sleeping. "Then said Jesus unto them plainly, Lazarus is dead," and he "had lain in the grave four days already."[49] But even so, his death was not a permanent state. Jesus said to Martha, Lazarus's sister, "I am the resurrection and the life . . . and whosoever liveth and believeth in me shall never die."[50] He tells us that If we believe in him, what he is teaching us and inviting us to do, that we, too, shall live again. Note that Jesus explicitly says "liveth and believeth." If we believe Jesus, we will live accordingly. In other words, if you believe in the resurrection, if we believe in redemption, we must live it and make it happen. If we believe him, we will do the works he has done.[51] Jesus said, "Lazarus come forth," and "he who was dead came forth."[52] As co-redeemers with Jesus in Christ, it is our responsibility and blessing to participate in this great work, to raise and redeem those whom we've lost.

What do we make of Jesus's charge? Is this simply a tale we tell ourselves to soothe our losses? With all we know about science and technology, is it even possible to redeem our dead? Will life be restored without effort on our part, or is this a call to action? If so, what practical actions do we take? What does this mean for queer bodies?

Redeeming our queer siblings means to give us back the life we never got to live. It means celebrating the trans woman in her fifties when she wears pink "Hello Kitty" rainboots because as a seven-year-old, she was told, "Boys don't wear that." It means celebrating a lesbian in her thirties who finally finds the love of her life, even after marrying a man and raising children with him. It's never too late to celebrate love. Redeeming queer folks means giving us back the debt that is owed—a life of love, authenticity, and flourishing unincumbered by violent threats, mistreatment, violence, and abuse. As for the queer children of God that we have lost to violence and/or suicide, it means we must raise them from the dead in all their queer celestial glory and giving them the opportunity to love and be loved by their communities. The redemption of queerness gives queer folks back our lives in every imaginable capacity. Our doctrine promises that everything that was stolen from us will be restored. And that isn't just Jesus' responsibility. It's the responsibility of every member of the body of Christ.

CHAPTER 4

Concerning The Family

Some critics think that The Church of Jesus Christ of Latter-day Saints has become so zealous and resolute in its definitions of "gender" and "family" that it will never support queer inclusivity. Others believe that there is no room for queer genders in Latter-day Saint worship because Mormon theology is immutably predicated on a strict cisgender, heterosexual binary. Some proclaim that gender is eternal and that all gender assignments are immutable decrees from God—to reject one's social role would be to reject God.

As previously stated, I see our theology as inherently queer-inclusive. I also believe that, for Latter-day Saint worship, policies, and rituals to reflect the queerness of Mormon theology, we must pave the way. We need to envision the possibility of queer inclusivity if it is ever to become a reality, including addressing *The Family: A Proclamation to the World*. We need to use our scriptures and proclamations as tools of love and inclusivity. If we are genuinely interested in "defending the family," we need to be clear about what we are actually defending.

Defending the Family

Many Latter-day Saints claim to be "defending the family" when they use *The Family: A Proclamation to the World*, scriptures, the General Handbook, or conference talks to justify excluding LGBTQ+ Latter-day Saints. While defending the family is an admirable goal and worthy endeavor, these good intentions often fall short when they fail to include all families. Furthermore, when someone claims to be "protecting the children" by excluding LGBTQ+ Latter-day Saints, they are actually vilifying some of God's most vulnerable children. If we truly want to protect children by defending the family, we needed to take a closer look at how current efforts to "defend the family" are actually harming children and families.

One problem with the way that "protecting the children by defending the family" is implemented is that it assumes that no children are queer. This is simply not true. Queer children and youth are in the pews listening to what their fellow Latter-day Saints say about queer people. When a congregant, bishop, leader, apostle, or prophet says that families need defense against queer people, these queer children are being portrayed as villains. "Defending the family" from other queer families and queer children pits children against children in a war that does not need to be fought. In a rush to defend the family, many Latter-day Saints vilify and reject queer children and shut them off from the blessing that comes with being part of a religious community. This is spiritual abuse. Our queer children and little ones are treated like invisible, yet acceptable, causalities in a battle where they were pointed at and called "the enemy of the family." Our queer children aren't being protected by current efforts to defend the family; they have become antagonists in this sad and misguided attempt to protect children.

I know what it feels like to be painted as the villain in a broken theology. It made me want to die. I cannot overstate how harmful it was to be taught that I was a threat to families. I was taught two very conflicting messages about my earthly purpose, and it almost ripped me apart. I had myself convinced that dying would be an act of charity.

First, as a Mormon woman, I was taught that motherhood was the most important thing I would ever do and that nothing else I accomplished would compare to bearing and raising children. Second, as a queer Mormon, I was taught I was inherently unfit to be a parent and that I would destroy families. Queerness was a threat to all families, especially my own.

When I was a young mother, there were days that I was convinced that the best thing a queer mother like me could do for her children was to die so that she could no longer harm them with her queerness. There was a little voice on my shoulder reminding me that my efforts would never be enough because who I am is inherently wrong. Even a lifetime performance of cisgender, heterosexual monogamy could not mask the queerness within. I would never be the mother or wife I was supposed to be, and that little voice on my shoulder had me convinced that leaving my husband and children behind would be an act of charity. Divorce would only hurt them more, and death seemed like a far more preferable way out.

These two conflicting messages have taken me years to untangle. I suppose it's easier to write about them now because I've learned to tell that little voice on my shoulder "no," and I'm so glad I did. I'm glad I learned to say "no" to the voices that made me want to die. I'm so glad I stayed because my queerness is not the evil thing that I was taught to fear. My queerness wasn't what was destroying my family's happiness. Believing my queerness was evil was what was destroying my family's happiness.

Every now and then, that voice comes back. It echoes in my mind the words of a hundred Sunday School lessons, General Conference talks, and folk doctrines praising motherhood while condemning queerness— as if the two are mutually exclusive. They aren't. However, that voice doesn't have the power it used to. Even with the burden of having to show that queer parents are just as good of parents as straight parents, I'm doing it. It's messy and riddled with mistakes, but I'm giving it my best. Once I learned to accept myself as I was—seeing my queerness as a gift and not a curse—our family was able to enjoy levels of happiness that I never dreamed of.

Our children, our queer little ones, shouldn't be burdened with thinking they are villains for wanting to grow up, marry a person of the same gender, and raise babies together. Our children should not be taught that it's wrong to identify as a different gender than the one that was assigned at birth. Vilifying the hopes and dreams of our queer children isn't how we defend families or protect children. Vilifying queer families and children is how family relationships are destroyed.

If we genuinely want to protect, nurture, and care for our queer little ones, we need to include them under the banner of "eternal families." We need to include and defend them with the same rigor that we defend cisgender and straight children. We need to use our theology, scriptures, and religion to better reflect the doctrine of inclusion predicated on the teachings of Christ.[1] Families are made up of so much more than gender or orientation. Families are made up of kindness, loyalty, inclusion, differences, and charity. Families are made of individual members, just like the body of Christ. No two members are meant to be the same, but each is valued for their unique contribution to the whole. Even members others have deemed to be weak and feeble are, in fact, indispensable.[2] We need to protect children and families as we would any other member of the body of Christ and love each member for its diverse and unique contribution to the family.

Individual Adaptation

The Family: A Proclamation to the World is a document produced by the First Presidency and Council of the Twelve Apostles. It was first read by President Gordon B. Hinckley as part of his message at the General Relief Society Meeting held September 23, 1995, in Salt Lake City, Utah.[3] It is not my intention to give a history of its existence, nor to refute its importance to many Latter-day Saints. Nor is it my intention to deliberate or speculate on the intentions of the authors of the document. It is my intention to demonstrate how the text of the document might be read and understood more charitably towards families that don't fit a hetero-nuclear family model.

The seventh paragraph of the document describes a stereotypical hetero-nuclear family. It describes a protective father and nurturing mother who rear their family in love and compassion.

> The family is ordained of God. Marriage between man and woman is essential to His eternal plan. Children are entitled to birth within the bonds of matrimony, and to be reared by a father and a mother who honor marital vows with complete fidelity. Happiness in family life is

most likely to be achieved when founded upon the teachings of the Lord Jesus Christ. Successful marriages and families are established and maintained on principles of faith, prayer, repentance, forgiveness, respect, love, compassion, work, and wholesome recreational activities. By divine design, fathers are to preside over their families in love and righteousness and are responsible to provide the necessities of life and protection for their families. Mothers are primarily responsible for the nurture of their children. In these sacred responsibilities, fathers and mothers are obligated to help one another as equal partners. Disability, death, or other circumstances may necessitate individual adaptation. Extended families should lend support when needed.[4]

This model of the family probably applies to many Latter-day Saint families without concern or dispute. However, even though this model may fit the experience of many Latter-day Saint families, it is not a perfect template for *all* Latter-day Saint families, and the authors explicitly noted that in the seventh paragraph.

The authors state that this model of the family was not the only type of family ordained by God. In the second to last sentence, the authors were inspired to permit accommodations for other circumstances. The text beautifully and prophetically states, "Disability, death, or **other circumstances may necessitate individual adaptation**. Extended families should lend support when needed." This sentence explicitly states that there are "other circumstances" which require "individual adaptation." What these "other circumstances" include are not explicitly stated in the document, but it is clear there are "other circumstances" which require adaptation. Here, there is room for the reader to interpret what is best for their own unique circumstances. Considering that there are many other Latter-day Saint families that don't fit this model, I'd say this clarification is more than a footnote; it's an essential part of the document.

Other circumstances could include a person who is gay. If a woman is gay and has no desire to marry a man and raise children with someone she does not love, we should consider the circumstances of the situation and allow individual adaptation as needed. Not only that, but the document also says, "families should lend support where needed." Nowhere in the document does it say a marriage between a woman and woman is not ordained of God. The text says, "Marriage between man and woman is essential to His [Heavenly Father] eternal plan." It could just as easily be the case that marriage between a woman and a woman is also essential to God's eternal plan even though it is not explicitly written in the text. Gay marriage simply isn't mentioned anywhere in the document.

Other circumstances could also include a trans woman married to a cisgender woman. The trans woman may have identified as a man prior to her transition, but after she transitions, the couple's biological offspring could have two mothers. Think of it: trans women show us that there are ways a lesbian couple can have their own biological offspring.

Other circumstances must include historical and genealogical polygamous families when such relationships are already sanctioned by the Church (e.g., Joseph Smith, Brigham Young, Wilford Woodruff). The future of polygamous families could include families with one mom and two dads, or one dad and three moms. This could include children with parents who have been divorced, who now have a biological mother and father and a stepmother and stepfather. Other circumstances might include single folks, asexual folks, or couples who have no desire to reproduce. Other circumstances could include a mixed-orientation marriage of an asexual man and heterosexual woman who is impregnated by a sperm donor.

"Individual adaptation" leaves the door open for many possibilities. While marriage between a man and woman is essential to God's plan, there are many other types of marriages and families which are just as essential to God's plan, even if they aren't explicitly stated in the document. "Other circumstances" implicitly means there is more than one type of family that is ordained of God, and we should lend support as needed.

I do not argue that my interpretation is what the authors of the document intended. I'm arguing what the text of the document says. If this is a divinely inspired document, then the text is what the authors were divinely inspired to write, and they wrote there are "other circumstances that necessitate individual adaptation." We don't know all the different types of families which could be included under "other circumstances," but there certainly is room for charity as we seek to be more Christlike. As stated in the last sentence, "Extended families should lend support when needed." Extended families should include neighbors, ward families, and the Church. In the body of Christ, we are all extended family. We should extend our support when possible, and one way of doing that is by reading the text more charitably to include a diversity of families, genders, orientations, and anatomies. The document does not say, "Don't be trans and don't be gay." The document says that circumstances may require adaptation, and we should be supportive as needed.

Gender is Eternal

Another common argument made against transgender folks is found in the second paragraph of *The Family: A Proclamation to the World*. The last sentence of the second paragraph reads, "Gender is an essential characteristic of individual premortal, mortal, and eternal identity and purpose."[5] For the sake of argument, let's assume that the concise view that "gender is eternal" is true within Mormon theology, even though it is not found in the Standard Works. Even if we grant that "gender is eternal," it does not follow that transgender and non-binary folks are contrary to God's laws. There are two ways to affirm the identity of transgender folks under the premise of gender being eternal.

The simplest explanation is that trans people do have a fixed, eternal gender which simply does not align with their body and/or gender assignment. Their spirit is "female," but they were misassigned as "male." A transgender person can claim to have an unchanged, eternal gender that is not in line with their assignment and still be consistent with the idea that "gender is eternal." It just so happens that their eternal gender is different from the gender they were assigned by their earthly community. The mistake is with their prescribed gender assignment, not with their gender identity. This argument could also be used to demonstrate why conversion therapy of trans folks won't work—conversion therapists are working against the body and spirit, not with the body and spirit.

However, while I can appreciate the argument for a fixed, eternal gender, it does not address the needs of gender-variant and gender-fluid folks. Of course, I do not blame transgender people who use this argument to legitimize their own experiences within the Mormon theological framework. It is a valuable and creative use of the Mormon narrative. I have no interest in creating division between two marginalized and oppressed groups in Mormonism. As I proceed, it is not my intent to delegitimize folks with a fixed gender, whether they are transgender or cisgender. It is my intent to argue that gender-variant, non-binary, and fluid gender identities are just as legitimate as fixed gender experiences.

The second argument I make for queer gender inclusivity requires we take a more careful look at the concept of "eternal." It is important to note that eternal does not mean static or unchanging. Eternal means existing forever, and to exist in Mormon theology is to be in a constant state of change. Some might even call it eternal progression. I am not the same yesterday as I am today, nor will I be the same person tomorrow that you are today. We all change biologically, cognitively, and spiritually. We are not stagnant. Yet, there is something about *me* that persists through various changes. Similarly, gender is not necessarily static and is also subject to change. Having an eternal gender does not mean an unchanged or static gender. If having a static gender were the intended meaning of "gender is eternal," the authors of the text could have written "gender is static," "gender never changes," "don't be trans," or "God doesn't want your gender to change," but that is not what the text says. The text says gender is an essential characteristic of an eternal existence and purpose. This allows a lot of room for interpretation and dynamic change.

For example, Mormonism teaches that God is eternal and has existed forever, yet Joseph Smith taught that God was once as we are now—a mortal being.[6] How could God always exist if God was once a mere human? This suggests that God has always existed in some capacity, yet this also would require God to undergo some sort of evolution into godhood. Hence, God is eternal but also changes. Change is an eternal constant in Mormon theology, and this sentiment could also be extended to gender. If God can change eternally, so can I. It is in my divine nature to do so. Not only that, but I can also change myself as many times as necessary.

Scriptures support the notion of a gender-diverse, gender-fluid God capable of complex morphology. The Spirit of God appears in the Bible as a burning bush, a dove, and even invisible.[7] If these verses are to be taken literally, God cannot be limited to a single male embodiment. I wonder what gender a burning bush is? If these verses are to be taken figuratively, then why should we take literally the idea that God's embodiment is limited to a cisgender male body? Whether you read these scriptures metaphorically or literally, we need to strongly reconsider the perceptions of God's embodiment. In Mormon theology, God is bound to a material embodiment, but that doesn't mean God's embodiment never changes. In fact, the opposite claim is made. God has a material embodiment that is capable of radical change, flexibility, morphology, and diverse interpretation. In the scriptures, God may appear as a man, a woman, an animal, or a plant and still be God. Consider the possibility that God appears in whatever way a viewer would meaningfully accept. That could be a man when appearing to Joseph Smith, or a burning bush when appearing to Moses.

From a Latter-day Saint perspective, Elder Erastus Snow stated, "If I believe anything God has ever said, anything about himself [. . .] I must believe that deity consists of man and woman."[8] It is unclear whether this is a description of one embodiment or multiple embodiments. If it is singular, then God is intersex. I prefer the interpretation that God is composed of many diverse embodiments. However, what is clear from scripture is that God is both male and female. Genesis states that both females and males are made in the image of God.[9] From this, we can reevaluate the image of God through our limited projections and conclude that God is both male and female; otherwise, women could not have been made in God's image. No matter where a person falls on the gender spectrum, according to the Bible, the image of God is both male *and* female, not male *or* female.

Furthermore, in Genesis, we are symbiotically created in the image of God, both male and female. People have read this passage of scripture and quickly assumed that this excludes queer, trans, or non-binary genders, but that hasty reading of scripture is incomplete. In Genesis, we also read about how God created night and day—two contrasting polarities separated from one another through lightness and darkness.[10] At first glance, it might seem like the division between day and night is a blunt self-evident distinction. However, in the following sentence, it states that God also created evening and morning.[11] Night and day, both necessary and lovely, are binaries resting at the ends of a broad spectrum. In between them are morning and evening. Yes, God created night and day, but God also created dawn and dusk. Dawn and dusk are no less godly than night and day simply because they are rare transitions. The same is true of humanity. God created man and woman—two lovely binaries made in the image of God. Yet in transition between them are non-binary bodies and spirits. Though we are rare, we are no less godly. We are the dawn and dusk of humanity. There is a spectrum of transitions between lightness and darkness, day and night, earth and water, man and woman. No matter where a person's body falls on the gender spectrum, we are all made in the image of God because God created more than binaries.

We are not only encouraged to become like God, but also promised in Psalms that we *are* gods and children of the Most High, joint-heirs with Christ, and that God is no respecter of persons.[12] No matter the gender identity, color of skin, physical embodiment, or anatomical differences that exist, we are an expression of the image of God. We cannot become God without embracing God's diverse morphology, including transgender, non-binary, genderqueer, intersex, gender variant, and especially gender-fluid folks like myself.

In contrast to our biblical narratives and Mormon theology, there are some Latter-day Saints who contend that a particular type of embodiment comes with a particular type of unchanging gender identity. They mistakenly read "gender is eternal" as "gender is static" or "gender is binary." If God is not limited by a particular embodiment, why should we limit ourselves and each other to a particular type of embodiment? Aren't we supposed to be like God? Likewise, if God's fullest image encompasses all of God's children, why limit a person to a particular gender expression when a person may prefer a fluid expression of their gender(s)? Of course, if people don't want to change anything about their gender, they shouldn't have to, but that doesn't mean people who identify with multiple genders should be limited to one expression of only one gender. Progressing into godhood means embracing bodies that are capable of radical and dynamic morphologies.

Confirmation through the Spirit

In Mormon theology, the Spirit plays an important role in our lives. The Spirit is how God communicates with us. The Spirit has the power to testify, reveal knowledge, redeem, and sanctify.[13] The Spirit can enlighten our minds and help us know what to do or which path to take.[14] The Spirit is also a comforter that dwells within us.[15] Our bodies are temples of the Holy Spirit when we are righteous.[16] When we are unrighteous, the Spirit ceases to be with us. As stated in 2 Nephi, "For the Spirit of the Lord will not always strive with man. And when the Spirit ceaseth to strive with man then cometh speedy destruction, and this grieveth my soul."[17] Righteousness invites the Spirit to dwell within us, and unrighteousness chases the Spirit away.

Quiet literally, the Spirit that dwells in me confirms truth through my body. Together, the body and spirit create the soul.[18] When my body is assaulted, my spirit is assaulted. When my spirit grieves, my body grieves. My material body and agency are two of the most powerful tools I am given.[19] I was deliberately given a body that I might have joy and delight in it. We could not achieve full happiness without a body.[20] By design, happiness is achieved when both body and spirit are in harmony with one another. If the spirit and body are separated from each other, we cannot receive a fulness of joy.[21] In the materiality of Mormonism, we *are* our bodies. Though the Spirit does not have a body of flesh and bone, the materiality of the Spirit is manifested through our flesh and bones.

My body can let me know when something is right and when something is wrong. When something is right, the Spirit speaks through euphoria, joy, delight, happiness, and peace. When something is wrong (or off), the Spirit speaks through dysphoria, misery, despair, and distress. When I deny the promptings of the Spirit, it might leave entirely.

Sadly, I know what it's like to alienate myself from the Spirit by neglecting its promptings. I cautiously share my own experience in the spirit of Elder Ballard's call to listen to the experiences of queer Latter-day Saints. As he so aptly stated, "We need to listen to and understand what our LGBT brothers and sisters are feeling and experiencing. Certainly, we must do better than we have done in the past."

Seven years ago, I stood in front of a bathroom mirror in my swimming suit, hating my body. I sobbed heavy, uncontrollable sobs. I ripped off my swimming suit, threw it in the trash, and laid on the shower floor while hot water pounded on my naked body. I hated my breasts. I hate the men who looked at them. I hated the women who judged me for them. I hate the men who freely walked around the swimming pool unashamed. I wanted them to feel just as shameful as I felt. I hated the indecency of my body. I hate the women who found my body obscene and protected their husband's virtuous thoughts by attacking my body. I hated the way I felt. I even hated the women I wanted. I hated myself for hating them.

I laid on the shower floor and thought about how I first taped my breasts down as a teenager just to keep them contained. Everything I tried so hard to keep under control with tape and virtuous thoughts was unleashed. I was queer—my gender, my body, my desires, my biology, my orientation—everything about me was queer, and no amount of tape was going to change that. My non-binary body and non-binary desires collided with a binary world, and I hated myself for it. The Spirit was absent. I was left alone, naked, and sobbing on the shower floor with nothing but my own self-loathing. The Spirit could not dwell with me when I was so heavily cloaked in the hatred of my queer body.

I can't remember how long that shower lasted. I stayed on the shower floor until scalding water turned frigid, and my heated rage turned into shivers. My body shook uncontrollably, from the trauma or the temperature I did not know. I turned off the water and laid on the shower floor, waiting for the Spirit to come back and speak to me.

Strangely, everything I had been taught about the Spirit was true. I was a living witness, and my body was a material testament. The Spirit couldn't dwell in this body, not because it was queer, but because I failed to listen to what the Spirit was trying to tell me through the promptings of dysphoria. I alienated myself from my body, and it hindered my access to the Spirit. Rejecting my queerness, suppressing my dysphoria, and denying my body are what led me to such extreme hatred. It wasn't my queerness or dysphoria that made me unworthy of the Spirit. It was the denial of my queerness, body and spirit, that alienated me from the Spirit. The Spirit couldn't tell me what I would not hear. I had to understand my dysphoria, not as a mental illness but a prompting from the Spirit. The sanctification of the Spirit could only happen by accepting my queerness, my body, my agency, and my desires as divine gifts and blessings.

I stopped crying and grew quiet. Instead of denying my dysphoria, I listened to my dysphoria. I listened to my body, and the Spirit came back. I was instructed to stop denying myself the joy I was promised.[22] The

Plan of Happiness is not a plan of shame, hatred, or self-denial. The Plan of Happiness is a plan of joy. The Spirit confirmed this truth through my body, and I acted upon those promptings. I called a surgeon, and within a week I was in the operating room.

When I awoke from the anesthesia, I was in considerable pain. My chest throbbed and screamed under the compression binder, but I didn't care. Physical pain couldn't hold a candle to the years of mental torture I had endured. I welcomed the pain and greeted it with a grateful heart.

Once I got home, I stood in front of the full-length mirror in my bedroom and carefully undressed. Each layer I removed brought me closer to seeing me, the new me, the real me. My robes dropped to the floor, exposing a wonderful, brilliant, bloody, bruised body that was wholly mine. The stitches laced through my purple flesh made me look like a science project gone awry, but I didn't mind. The tubes and wires which were still attached to my body didn't bother me in the slightest. My chest was black and blue. I was a beautiful disaster in desperate need of a shower, but I was overjoyed.

It was only when I allowed myself to fully feel my gender dysphoria that I was able to create my gender euphoria. Is this what it meant to be transfigured and crowned with glory? I felt like I was truly created and that I might have joy. My body and spirit were unified. Not only did I feel worthy, but I also felt glory.[23] I was filled with glory. The earth was filled with glory. The heavens were filled with glory. The harmony of both my body and spirit opened the doors to more love, kindness, and charity than I had ever imagined.

My new body wasn't a defilement as some might imbue. I wasn't ruined, soiled, unclean, or polluted. Dysphoria wasn't a sign of mental illness. The Spirit was letting me know something was very wrong, and I had the power to make it right. My new body was a transfigured body filled with goodness, compassion, and love. My body was blessed with holy powers, and the Spirit confirmed this truth through both gender dysphoria and gender euphoria. And what greater confirmation could be had than a witness from God through the Spirit?[24]

CHAPTER 5

Concerning Sexuality and Creation

A common argument made against homosexuals is that they can't enter the highest degree of celestial glory because they cannot procreate. According to a reductive interpretation of Mormon theology, if homosexuals cannot create their own biological offspring, then they cannot have eternal increase.[1] This argument has several problems. First, some forms of same-sex reproduction are already possible with our current levels of technology, with more opportunities on the horizon. Second, this argument fails to account for the many families composed of parents and children who are not biologically related but are still promised celestial glory through adoptive sealing ordinances. Adoption is a legitimate form of eternal increase in Mormonism. Third, our own scriptures teach that procreation involves much more than cisgender heterosexual copulation. Eternal increase is more than biological reproduction. Fourth, godly creation is collaborative, and in collaborative creation, not all participants must be parents or even married to rear children. And finally, the primary focus of creation should be on *theosis*, immortality, eternal life, and the creation of Gods, not the gender of the persons who are collaborating in this godly process.

Technological Creation

Reproductive technologies are changing the landscape of gender, sexuality, and procreation. The last century has brought an explosion of advancements in reproductive technology. Many religions, including Latter-day Saints, have embraced technologies that permit their members to successfully create biological families. As stated in the *General Handbook*, "When needed, reproductive technology can assist a married woman and man in their righteous desire to have children."[2]

Latter-day Saints have exceptionally positive views of procreation. Mormon scriptures, prophets, and temple rituals teach that not only are we encouraged to reproduce, but we are also commanded to multiply and replenish the earth, then nurture those children into godhood.[3] Using the power of procreation does not alienate us from God, but rather enables us to become co-creators with God in a divine plan of eternal increase. Creation is a divine partnership.[4] Church leaders have counseled members to seek inspiration from God as they use their individual agency to bring children into the world. The *General Handbook* states, "However, this is a personal matter that is ultimately left to the judgment and prayerful consideration of a lawfully married man and woman."[5] Much of how members of the Church choose to procreate is left to the agency and inspiration of the persons involved.

Many people encounter difficult challenges when procreating, but reproductive technologies have allowed parents to overcome many obstacles to engage the power of creation. Some forms of assisted reproductive technology include:

- **Artificial insemination:** the deliberate induction of sperm into a uterus in hopes of achieving pregnancy when sexual intercourse isn't a viable option.

- **In vitro fertilization:** method of assisted reproduction that involves the extraction of an egg and sperm from the parents. Fertilization of egg and sperm is done manually in a laboratory dish. The embryo is then transferred back into a uterus for gestation.

- **In vitro fertilization with three biological parents:** used to prevent the passing on of mitochondrial disorders to their offspring. The biological parents donate their egg and sperm much as they do in the process of in vitro fertilization; however, a third donor contributes healthy mitochondria that replaces the defective mitochondria of the first donor's egg. The altered embryo is transferred into a uterus for gestation. The child is the biological offspring of three parents—two egg donors and one sperm donor.[6]

- **Surrogacy:** an embryo is produced via in vitro fertilization, but the uterus used for gestation is of a willing and consenting surrogate.[7] This process was recently used by a 58-year-old woman in Texas, who was a surrogate for her daughter and son-in-law who had encountered many difficulties conceiving their own child. Even though the grandmother already experienced menopause, her uterus was still functional, so she offered her womb to gestate her granddaughter. In an interview, she said, "It's such a blessing I can do this for my daughter."[8]

- **Uterus transplant:** a healthy uterus is implanted into a cisgender woman with a faulty, dysfunctional, or absent uterus. In 2014, a healthy baby was delivered by a cisgender woman who received a uterus transplant. The doctor who performed the transplant said, "The baby is fantastic, but it is even better to see the joy in the parents."[9] Hundreds of uterus transplants are taking place right now, giving hope to more couples who wish to conceive.

Eventually, uterus transplants may allow transgender women to gestate children too. It seems fitting for individuals who were assigned male at birth to aspire to motherhood when Latter-day apostles teach "the highest and noblest work in this life is that of a mother" and motherhood "is the highest, holiest service to be assumed by mankind."[10] Please note that motherhood is to be assumed by *mankind*. The semantics implicitly leaves room for mothers of various anatomies. Why shouldn't a woman who was assigned male aspire to motherhood if she decides it is her noblest work? Why does biology prevent her from pregnancy any more than a cisgender woman who struggles with infertility? If a transgender woman desires motherhood as her holiest work, who are we to prevent her service to the community? When all technological barriers have been removed, why not simply allow parents to engage in parenthood as their holiest work according to their skills and desires instead of an imposed gender assignment?

Elder M. Russell Ballard also said, "There is no one perfect way to be a good mother. Each situation is unique. Each mother has different challenges, different skills and abilities ... what matters is that a mother loves her children deeply." [11] When it comes to rearing children, according to Ballard, the most important qualification should be love for the child. The primary concern is not whether or not she has a functioning uterus, not if the child was adopted, not if the mother has a penis and testicles, but rather that she loves her children deeply. This need not even be a gendered idea. In *The Family: A Proclamation to the World*, we read, "Parents have a sacred duty to rear their children in love and righteousness, to provide for their physical and spiritual needs, and to teach them to love and serve one another, observe the commandments of God, and be law-abiding citizens wherever they live." [12] The most important role of all parents is that they love their children, provide for their needs, and nurture them into godhood through love. All of God's commandments hinge on the principle of love. [13]

Keep in mind that it is already possible for a biological offspring to share DNA with three parents—two egg donors and one sperm donor. Right now, it is possible for two cisgender women to have biological offspring who share both their genetic material. The relationship dynamics of the parents may vary. Two bisexual cisgender women and their cisgender husband could produce their own biological child. Or a lesbian couple might use a sperm donor to produce their own biological child. Or all participants could be agender and asexual, with one of them being impregnated via in vitro fertilization. Regardless of the relationship dynamics of the biological parents, their offspring will share genetic material from all three.

In time, I suspect, there will be technology that allows two cisgender fathers to create their own offspring, though this may take considerably more time to achieve.[14] Perhaps, in time, technologists and physicians might create external wombs for parents who want to gestate their offspring with more safety and control than a deformed uterus which might spontaneously abort or miscarry the fetus.[15] The future holds many possibilities for biological reproduction.

Some of these reproductive technologies may seem controversial today, and there are certainly ethical concerns to address. But keep in mind that artificial insemination, in vitro fertilization, and surrogacy were once considered highly controversial and are now accepted as useful means of assisted reproduction for many faithful Latter-day Saint families. The General Handbook affirms that "children conceived by artificial insemination or in vitro fertilization are born in the covenant."[16]

However, what is perhaps even more exciting is that transgender folks have shown us that homosexual reproduction is already possible. Depending on the anatomy of the persons involved, a transgender man and a cisgender man can already reproduce their own biological offspring together. Transgender men who desire fatherhood as gestational dads can even nurse their babies in a practice called "chestfeeding."[17] Similarly, a lesbian couple composed of a transgender woman and cisgender woman can also produce their own biological offspring. It is also possible for trans women to breastfeed.[18]

As reproductive technologies rapidly change, some might see this as a threat to traditional theology. These technologies, though, are a manifestation of our deepest desires to be like God. Social and technological boundaries are being breached to allow parents the ability to create biological families of their own. As technology improves, it is my hope that we will embrace diverse families with the common and central intent to create, rear, and love children just as much as our Heavenly Parents do.

Adoptive Creation

Mormons also have considerably favorable views about adoption. There are no doctrinal limitations on legal adoption in The Church of Jesus Christ of Latter-day Saints, and in most circumstances, children can be sealed to their adoptive parents. In Mormon theology, adoptive sealings are just as legitimate as birth in the covenant. "Children who are not born in the covenant can become part of an eternal family by being sealed to their natural or adoptive parents. These children receive the same right to blessing as if they had been born in the covenant." [19] Not only that, but adoptive parents have also been praised by Mormon authorities for their devotion to raising God's children. Ezra Taft Benson once said of adoptive parents that, "We salute these wonderful couples for the sacrifices and love you have given to those children you have chosen to call your own." [20] Adoption is a form of parenthood that is legitimate and celebrated in Mormonism.

Through sealing power, adoptive parents have children in the eternities whom they did not biologically reproduce. Adoptive families show us that sealing power can bind families regardless of shared genetic material. The ability or inability to biologically reproduce with your partner is not what makes a family a celestial family. Sealings, not reproductive anatomy, make families eternal. Furthermore, it is not biology that stands in the way of queer families being sealed. It is our collective inability to imagine that queer families created through adoption are just as godly as families created through biology. The rejection of queer adoptive families is a failure on our part that demonstrates we do not fully believe our existing doctrine of sealing power.

In a way, we are all adoptive parents. Adoptive parents have been entrusted with the stewardship to love and rear children, just as biological parents have been entrusted to be stewards over our Heavenly Parents' children. Even children born to biological parents are a kind of stewardship. In Mormon theology, we are all children of Heavenly Parents, and they have entrusted our growth and development to one another. My children are not simply my children; they are also children of God, and I am entrusted by Heavenly Mother to be their earthly mother. In this sense, we are all adoptive parents, no matter how our children came to us. We are trusted to be stewards for each other by the grace of loving Heavenly Parents. This divinely inspired stewardship is not limited by biology but by our ability to rear children in love and charity.

Queer Creation

I was first introduced to queerness of procreation in Mormon theology by Taylor Petrey, a professor of Religious Studies and Women's Studies at Kalamazoo College. In his essay "Toward a Post-Heterosexual Mormon Theology,"[21] Petrey illuminates a beautiful precedent for queer procreation in Mormon theology. His work, which I highly recommend, has greatly influenced my own views of how Gods create in Mormon theology.[22]

As Petrey points out in his paper, godly creation is far queerer than we have previously imagined. In the creation of Adam and Eve, there is no account of cisgender, heterosexual copulation being a necessary means of reproduction.

> Both spiritual and material formation takes place without any sexual union. Furthermore, males alone perform the creation of Adam's body. Even Eve is "reproduced" from a male body with the help of other males. The Lord penetrates the body of Adam and creates Eve. The capacity for Adam's body to reproduce by means of another male provides scriptural precedent in the foundational story of humanity to the variety of possibilities available for Latter-day Saints to conceive of reproduction independent of heterosexual union.[23]

In the story outlined in scripture, the creation of humanity, even a woman, was produced by three men: God the Eternal Father, his son Jesus Christ, and Adam.[24] What a queer thought to think of three men creating a woman! Now, it could be the case that Heavenly Mother was involved in the creative process, but if She were, there was no direct account of it written in scripture, nor is her role explicitly stated in Latter-day Saint temple ritual.

However, even if Heavenly Mother and/or other women were involved in creating Eve, the process is still queer when a woman was created from a man's rib. If they share the same karyotype (chromosomes), that could make Adam a trans man (XX) and Eve a cis woman (XX). Although the inverse could also be true. Adam could be thought of as a cis man (XY), making Eve a trans woman (XY). In either case, the creation of a woman from a man's body comes with biologically queer implications and considerations.

However, what I find even more interesting is the godly creation of Jesus' body through Mary. According to Christian tradition, Mary, the mother of Jesus, was a virgin. When the angel told her she was to conceive, she replied, "How shall this be, seeing I know not a man?" Here, Mary explicitly asks how can she be impregnated if she's never been with a man? She is asking the same question that critics of homosexual couples are asking. If cisgender homosexual men and women aren't procreating through copulation, how on earth are they going to have children? The angel answers somewhat ambiguously, "The Holy Ghost shall come upon thee, and the power of the Highest will overshadow thee." [25] If Mary can be impregnated without knowing a man, why can't a cis lesbian be impregnated without knowing a man?

Let us also consider this queer situation from the point of Joseph, Mary's earthly husband. Mary, the mother of Jesus, was a virgin and impregnated independent of Joseph. He "knew her not till she had brought forth her firstborn son." [26] However, Joseph was married to Mary, even though she was pregnant with a child that was not biologically his. Under the law, she could have been cast out and put to death. Yet, she was not called to repentance, but instead praised as "beautiful," "precious," and "chosen." [27] Jesus' mother became pregnant by means other than her husband, and she was praised for it.

What are we to do with these passages of scripture? What are we to make of Jesus' family? Should Mary, the mother of Jesus, be excluded from the highest degree of celestial glory because she didn't reproduce via earthly, cisgender, heterosexual copulation with a fertile cisgender male? Does the letter of the law apply to Mary? Is she to be called to repentance for bearing a child that wasn't her earthly husband's? Or is this a case of "other circumstances" that require "individual adaptation" to bring a Savior into the world? According to *The Family: A Proclamation to the World*, we should "lend support as needed," not condemn the conception of Jesus.

If Mary was indeed a virgin, as Mormon authorities have affirmed and disconfirmed, there was no copulation involved in the conception and creation of Jesus.[28] The creation of Jesus did not require sex. It is nonsensical to assume that creation in the highest degree of celestial glory would necessarily require cis male and cis female intercourse when the Savior of the world was created independent of copulation.

Mary's conception of Jesus shows us there is more than one way to produce offspring without intercourse. The words "traditional marriage" or "traditional family" certainly don't apply to Joseph, Mary, and Jesus. The Holy Family was undoubtably queer. Let's look at the dynamics of Jesus' family while removing the sexed-focused assumptions of how children are made and reared.

Jesus' Heavenly Mother and Father allowed the conception of Jesus through their daughter, Mary. She was impregnated by the Holy Spirit under the direction of her Heavenly Father—even though she had no husband. Mary then became the earthly mother and spirit sister of Jesus. Jesus was also the spirit brother and stepson of his father, Joseph. Jesus had two fathers—Heavenly Father, who instigated his non-copulatory conception, and Joseph, his earthly stepfather who raised him. Jesus also had two mothers, Mary and Heavenly Mother. I'd like to believe that his Heavenly Mother and his earthly mother were bound or sealed to one another as both mother and daughter, and as sister wives raising their common son, Jesus. I imagine the love Mary had for her son Jesus was tantamount to the love Heavenly Mother had for her son Jesus. I imagine they both suffered the pains of a grieving mother as they both watched their son being crucified. Indeed, two mothers wept as they watched their son being tortured and killed. Jesus came from a queer family, and each of them played a significant role in the creation of the Savior.

Mary is the heroine of the story. Her story defies all known boundaries of cisgender, heterosexual reproduction, as she birthed a God in an act of divine creation. She defied the letter of the law, and Joseph lent support as needed. She has shown us that godly procreation can happen independently of heterosexual copulation. Once we remove the sexed-focused lens of procreation, we can begin to see Jesus' family in all its queerness as a group of people heavily invested in providing a Savior for the world. Mary was more than a chosen vessel; she taught us that the creation of a God is a communal and queer experience.

Collaborative Creation

In Latter-day Saint culture, people who are voluntarily single or childless are also "queer." When Mormon theology puts such a heavy emphasis on marriage and procreation, can you even be afaithful Latter-day Saint if you do not desire an eternity of reproduction and parenthood? Regardless of gender and sexual orientation, I contend that even people who don't want to be parents in the eternities can still be a valuable part of divine creation.[29] As demonstrated by the creation of Adam and Eve and the birth of Jesus, godly creation is collaborative, and not everyone will have the same role.

For example, in the creation of Jesus Christ, Heavenly Mother did not nurse him as an infant; Mary did that. Joseph was not the parent providing genetic material, but he certainly had a hand in raising him. It's also worth noting that John the Baptist played an essential role in preparing the way for Jesus. Furthermore, after his death, Jesus also relied on his disciples to share the story of Christ. The creation of the Savior is a collaborative effort. It really does take a village to birth a Savior, even though not all participants are married or parents. The collective effort of creating Christ included many hands, and everyone had different talents to contribute.

As previously discussed, there is room for everyone in the body of Christ, and not all members need to be child-bearers or parents. Each member is a valued member, and we all have different talents to contribute to the body of Christ. Unmarried and childless members who wish to remain childless or unmarried should also be welcomed into the highest degree of glory, even though their contributions to "eternal increase" are not of a biologically parental nature. Their contribution as aunts and uncles, godmothers and godfathers, friends and neighbors, or decent citizens doing good things help make the world a better place. Their roles and contributions are equally important in the collaborative creation of Christ—just as important as another biological or adoptive parent. It takes a village to rear our children, and everyone in the village is important and valuable.

I suggest we look beyond our assumptions of biological procreation and consider godly creation as a form of collaborative creation. One of God's purposes is to bring to pass the immortality of humanity.[30] The world was created for this very purpose. If you are working toward the joy and immortality of humanity through love and charity, you are doing God's work. There is no need to limit godly creation to human reproduction. Collaborative creation includes everyone who is working toward the creation of godhood and glorified communities.

•

Godly Creation

Godly creation is so much more than cisgender, heterosexual copulation. Godly creation is just that: the creative process used by gods. When I consider the most divine creation possible, what we must all aspire toward, I cannot help but harken back to *theosis*. The most beautiful and queerest of creations is godhood—a future of our own making through a queer Christ. This should be the type of creation we direct our attention towards, not the gender of the persons doing the creating.

As I think about the creation of Gods, I am inspired by the story of Mary, the mother of Jesus Christ. She birthed a God so great he was able to take on the sins and sorrows of the world to make us whole. Mary birthed a Savior. Without her, there would be no Atonement. May we be like Mary and birth a god together. May we be like Joseph and support each other under queer circumstances. May we be like John and prepare the way for Christ. May we be like Jesus' disciples and share the good news of the Christ beyond death. May we be like Jesus and reconcile with one another through the Atonement. As disciples of Jesus, we create the body of Christ. In so doing, we also become co-creators *of* God and *with* God, just as Mary did. She was both the co-creator *of* God and *with* God. As members of the body of Christ, we take on the role of Mary, Joseph, John, and Jesus in an effort to transform humanity into something godly.

In Nephi we read, "For if there be no Christ there be no God; and if there be no God we are not, for there could have been no creation. But there is a God, and he is Christ, and he cometh in the fullness of his own time."[31] Here we read that God and Christ are inseparable, and as previously demonstrated, we are the body of Christ.[32] In Mormon theology, there is no God without us and no us without God. We are co-eternal with God.[33] We exist in a symbiotic relationship with God where we are both growing and developing together. Granted, God is significantly more developed than we are, but this is a difference only of *degree*, not *kind*. The scriptures clearly state that God is Christ, and we, too, are the body of Christ. We are members of the body of Christ with Jesus on a path to godhood, and that is our ultimate co-creation.

Mary will always hold a special place in my heart as an exemplar of godly creation. Her story defies known boundaries of reproduction, as she birthed a God in an act of divine creation. If we, as the body of Christ, are going to birth a God by becoming gods ourselves, we should look to Mary as the creator of Christ. She shatters our limited knowledge of conception, creation, sexuality, reproduction, and divinization. She is the heroine who compels us to reconsider the boundaries of impossibility by making the impossible possible.

Eternal Increase

While it is often assumed "eternal increase" is tantamount to biological reproduction, I contend that eternal increase is significantly more. Eternal increase is a priesthood blessing promised to those in the highest degree of celestial glory. Those who do not enter the new and everlasting covenant of marriage cannot have increase. As we have learned in Doctrine and Covenants,

> In the celestial glory there are three heavens or degrees; And in order to obtain the highest, a man must enter into this order of the priesthood [meaning the new and everlasting covenant of marriage]; And if he does not, he cannot obtain it. He may enter into the other, but that is the end of his kingdom; he cannot have an increase.[34]

Here, we read that increase is a matter of sealed marriage, not biology. This is also not just any type of marriage. This is the new and everlasting covenant of marriage, also called plural marriage—an issue I will address in my Queer Polygamy model in the following chapter. In these scriptures, "increase" is a blessing for those in the highest degree of celestial glory. Joseph Smith expanded on the notion of eternal increase by saying,

> Except a man and his wife enter into an everlasting covenant and be married for eternity, while in this probation, by the power and authority of the Holy Priesthood, they will cease to increase when they die; that is, they will not have any children after the resurrection. But those who are married by the power and authority of the priesthood in this life, and continue without committing the sin against the Holy Ghost, will continue to increase and have children in the celestial glory.[35]

Note here that the blessing of eternal increase in the next life is not dependent on the couple's mortal fertility. The promise of eternal increase is made to those who are married by priesthood authority. This means that a fertile cisgender, heterosexual couple will be denied the blessing of eternal increase if they are not sealed. The fertility of the participants is irrelevant to whether or not they have eternal increase. Yet, the Church does not bar infertile cisgender heterosexual couples from being sealed because they are unable to reproduce. We seal them together and promise them eternal increase even when we don't know what that will look like.

It makes no more sense to prohibit homosexual couples from being sealed to each other for the same reason it makes no sense to deny infertile, cisgender, hetersexual couples. Theoretically, if a cisgender homosexual couple were to be sealed by priesthood power and authority, they would have the blessing of eternal increase regardless of their biology—the same as infertile couples who are sealed in the temple. We don't have to know how "eternal increase" will happen to promise it. The eternal increase of cisgender homosexual couples could be a technological process, adoptive process, queer process, collaborative process, or godly process. Whatever their increase is, it too counts as "eternal increase." The promise of eternal increase in the next life is a priesthood promise that extends beyond current notions of biological fertility.

Furthermore, if the ability to reproduce biologically is truly the qualifier for a temple sealing and eternal increase, there should be no reason why a fertile couple composed of a transgender woman and transgender man should be prohibited from a temple sealing. Under this premise, eternal increase is a matter of biological reproduction. Furthermore, all infertile couples, queer or otherwise, should be disallowed from the temple, and all fertile couples, queer or otherwise, should be sealed in the temple. Logically, this would also mean that people who have had a vasectomy or tubal ligation should have their temple sealings canceled—at least until they can get their operation reversed. Furthermore, a woman after menopause would also need to have her sealing canceled on account of her infertility. However, I find this biological, legalistic approach to eternal increase unhelpful, unloving, and uninspiring.

I am inspired by the ideas of technological creation, adoptive creation, queer creation, collaborative creation, and godly creation. The blessings of eternal increase can be made available to all people if we so choose to embrace a theology of inclusive creation. The eternal increase of queer couples and queer families is not limited by biology or God. It is limited by us. God has already revealed through both scripture and science that there are many ways we might have eternal increase. Even our single and childless siblings can share in the blessings of eternal increase when we are all a part of the same divine family. It is time we embrace these various forms of creation, beyond sexuality, in a divine partnership to lift one another up together.

CHAPTER 6

Concerning Polygamy

During the early formation of the Church, Mormons proclaimed plural marriage as a requirement to reach the highest degree of celestial glory.[1] Mormons didn't simply have queer beliefs about marriage and sexuality; they lived those beliefs. Many of my polygamous ancestors lived the principle of plurality and entered into queer relationships with one another. My fourth great-grandmother, Amanda Barnes Smith, was sealed to Joseph Smith after his martyrdom. Brigham Young stood in as proxy, sealing Amanda to Joseph Smith.[2] My husband's fourth great aunt, Fanny Alger, was Joseph's first, and perhaps most controversial, plural wife.[3] Polygamy was such a queer form of sexuality and marriage that it provoked retaliation not just from angry mobs but also from the US government, which threatened to seize their assets. Wilford Woodruff, third president of the Church, released a manifesto with the intention of ending polygamy, but the practice persisted. Plural marriage could not be so easily abandoned when plurality bound them together as a "peculiar people."[4] Mormons were willing to endure ostracism in favor of their queer principles and beliefs.

I'm confident that every aspect of the Church has been touched by our controversial history with the practice of polygamy. Polygamy's omnipresence in Mormon theology makes it important to address in this book. The focus of this chapter is not to give a history or analysis of Mormon polygamy. My focus is to give a new theological approach to the principle of plurality while leaving room for a wide variety of marital and sexual preferences. The Queer Polygamy model presented in this chapter is intended to be an inspiring way to reimagine polygamy as a principle of plural love and sealings, not necessarily shared marital or sexual partners. Essentially, if members are given the liberty to engage in plural sealings, they can fulfill the law of plurality while also remaining in a heterosexual, monogamous relationship, if that is their desire.

Preliminaries

Let's begin with definitions. Polyandry means one woman married to multiple men. Polygyny means one man married to multiple women. Polygamy or plural marriage means any combination of polyandry and polygyny. And monogamy means having only one sexual and/or marital partner. A common form of monogamy is serial monogamy or having one monogamous partner at a time. In Mormonism, serial monogamy can be a form of polygamy when someone is sealed eternally to multiple partners that they have had monogamously. For example, President Russell M. Nelson is sealed to both of his wives, even though he was never married to them both at the same time.[5] According to Mormon theology, he will be a practicing polygamist in the highest degree of celestial glory.

Plural sealings are generally reserved for men and are very patriarchal. For women, plural sealings are only permitted if the woman is deceased. A living woman and her monogamous husbands are not afforded plural sealings until all members of the plural marriage are dead. Yet men may be sealed to all or any of their legal serial wives, so long as the women were not sealed to other men.[6] Polygamy has predominately been patriarchal, with restrictions placed on women's desires and participation. Polygamy has rarely, if ever, been practiced equitably in Mormonism. Early Mormon polygamy was exceptionally complicated and steeped in authoritarianism, sexism, racism, and coercion. I agree with many critiques of early Mormon polygamy involving underage participants, violence, manipulation, and deceit. Early Mormon polygamy hurt many people, and I have no intention of making apologetic arguments to defend such immoral implementations of polygamy.

In response, some Mormon feminists have advocated for the complete removal and disavowal of polygamy. This, however, would mandate monogamy as the only godly form of marriage. This is simply replacing one oppressive mandate with another. It's another case of the oppressed becoming the oppressor. Any future policy concerning sexual and marital practices should value individual agency while also working toward a safe environment where participants' desires and values are respected— be they monogamous, polygamous, straight, or queer.

The morality of a marriage cannot be reduced exclusively to whether or not it is monogamous or polygamous. I can list many mistakes and abuses in monogamous marriages, but that doesn't make monogamy inherently wrong. If a child is being abused by a parent, it doesn't matter if that parent is in a monogamous or polygamous marriage. Abuse is wrong regardless. Similarly, a marriage composed of a heterosexual or homosexual couple is not what makes it moral. If a child is being abused, it doesn't matter if the parent is heterosexual, bisexual, asexual, or homosexual. A relationship's morality is not a matter of monogamy, polygamy, homosexuality, or heterosexuality. A relationship's morality should be judged upon the values of love, life, joy, and agency.

Plurality, at its core, is the idea that we are capable of loving more than one person. To reduce the principle of plurality and plural sealings exclusively to sexual relationships would be a sore disservice to the richness of Mormon theology. Sealing power reaches beyond a single couple from parent to child, sibling to sibling, friend to friend. Limitations on sealings on account of gender seem counterintuitive to Mormonism's ultimate goal to seal the whole human family together. Shouldn't we all have the blessing of being sealed to all our loved ones regardless of gender?

Sadly, current Latter-day Saint sealing practices still support a cisgender, heterosexual, patriarchal approach to plural marriage. Current policy treats members differently, as different genders are given different expectations and limitations of whom they may be sealed to. Even though Latter-day Saint temple sealings are patriarchal and androcentric, temple practices and policies have dramatically changed over the years. It stands to reason that policies, wording, ritual, and even plural sealings will continue to evolve to include the equitable participation of not only women, but of all genders and orientations.

Queer Polygamy

According to many accounts of Latter-day Saint theology, polygamy, also called celestial marriage, is necessary for the highest degree of celestial glory. The Doctrine and Covenants teaches us that celestial marriage and the continuation of the human family will enable us to become Gods because we will have endless, everlasting increase.[7] Doctrine and Covenants gives a direct warning that, if we do not abide by the law of plural marriage, we cannot attain this glory.[8] Likewise, prophets have stated that *theosis* and plural marriage are intimately intertwined. Brigham Young, the most notable advocate for mandated polygamy, stated, "The only men who become Gods, even the sons of God, are those who enter into polygamy."[9] However, he also wrote, "... if you desire with all your hearts to obtain the blessings which Abraham obtained you will be polygamists at least in your faith."[10] It is interesting that he uses the words "at least in faith." Was this to suggest that if a man cannot practice polygamy on earth, he will in heaven? Or is this to suggest a man may never enter into a polygamous marriage but may live the spirit of polygamy in his heart? Later, Wilford Woodruff recorded in his journal that "President Young said there would be men saved in the Celestial Kingdom of God with one wife with Many wives & with No wife at all."[11] Woodruff also wrote, "Then President Young spoke 58 Minutes. He said a Man may Embrace the Law of Celestial Marriage in his heart & not take the Second wife & be justified before the Lord."[12] What is to be made of these statements? How can one embrace the spirit of polygamy, the Law of Celestial Marriage, but remain monogamous with one wife or even no wives?

I will refer to the sex-focused, androcentric, patriarchal, heteronormative model of polygyny as the *Standard Model*. At a glance, the Standard Model is highly problematic. Though the Standard Model tends to dominate the discourse, a more creative interpretation of what the spirit of polygamy includes may offer new insight into what celestial relationships might look like. I'm suggesting a way to reconcile diverse desires for celestial marriage under a new model that I call *Queer Polygamy*, which encompasses the spirit of polygamy without mandating any specific marital relations. I will begin my analysis with an expository of the Standard Model of polygamy followed by an expository of the Queer Polygamy Model and demonstrate how plural marriage may be redeemed to accommodate diverse relationships and desires, as Brigham Young suggests. I will then point out five common concerns with the Standard Model of polygamy and explain how the Queer Polygamy Model addresses them.

The Standard Model of polygamy is characterized as one man having multiple wives. The man will continue to increase in power and dominion according to the number of wives and children he accumulates. This means he is eternally sealed to all his wives and children as a God, like Heavenly Father, who also must have entered into plural marriage at some point. To attain the highest degree of celestial glory and have eternal increase, a man must enter into polygamy. The Standard Model focuses exclusively on the man, or patriarch, with little regard to what others, especially women and children, desire.

This projection of God and godhood is problematic for many reasons. This view paints an androcentric and domineering picture of what polygamy might look like. Additionally, it makes God a patriarchal monarch whose power and glory aren't shared with his family and community but exercised at their expense. If God evolved into godhood as a lone patriarch, then his power is not holy, but tyrannical. This patriarchal model of God, polygamy, sealings, celestial glory, and heaven are not a vision of glory most of us would aspire to as Saints in Zion. The Standard Model also neglects the Law of Consecration, the doctrine of *theosis* for all, and other communal practices of Zion. The people of Zion live together as equals, having one heart and one mind.[13] The Saints of Zion *together* enjoy the highest degree of glory and happiness that can be received in this life and, if they are faithful, in the world to come. Zion can be thought of as a template for how gods become gods. Yet, the Standard Model of polygamy doesn't resemble anything Latter-day Saints might want to strive for. The God of the Standard Model sounds more like a venture capitalist accruing wives and children for self-glorification rather than a collective group of Saints living in pure love with one another. Community, diversity, nuance, and even sometimes, consent are lost in this simplistic narrative.[14]

I believe queer theology is ripe with possibilities to reconcile our diverse aspirations towards Zion in a model I call *Queer Polygamy*, a model which can accommodate a potentially infinite number of marital, sexual, romantic, non-romantic, and celestial relationships. The words *Queer Polygamy* almost seem redundant. Polygamy is inherently queer according to contemporary monogamous marital expectations. It is, by western standards, a deviation from the norm. The words *Queer Polygamy* may also seem to imply that a person must necessarily be a member of the LGBTQ+ community for these ideas to apply, but this is not the case. Rest assured, heterosexual monogamous couples are an important subset under the umbrella of Queer Polygamy, just as Brigham Young suggested. A person with many, one, or no spouses may be included in this model. The use of the word *queer* in Queer Polygamy is to signify a more thoughtful and thorough interpretation of polygamy which would be inclusive of such diversity and that many of its manifestations would be rightly considered queer. You may initially find this model strangely foreign, but I believe it is in harmony with Mormon theology, both logically and practically, as both scripture and past prophets have taught. The word *polygamy* is used to specifically signify the plurality of relationships we engage in and that celestial marriage and eternal sealings include far more practices than heterosexual monogamy or androcentric polygyny. Eternal sealings among the Saints are inherently plural. Queer Polygamy is not opposed to Latter-day Saint theology, but rather the fulfillment of the all-inclusive breadth that Latter-day Saint theology has to offer.

The Standard Model of polygamy is problematic for many reasons, as many Latter-day Saint feminists and queer theologians have pointed out. I will review five of the most common problems with the Standard Model, then demonstrate how they might be reconciled by adopting the Queer Polygamy Model. The five common concerns are that the Standard Model does not leave room for the following types of people: (1) monogamous couples (2) women and other genders who desire plural marriage (3) singles and/or asexuals (4) homosexual relationships (5) plural parental sealings.

First, an unnuanced reading of Doctrine and Covenants section 132 appeals to a patriarchal and androcentric model of polygyny built upon a hierarchy of men who will be given women, also called virgins, as if they were property.[15] This exclusively polygynous model is a major concern for women who do not wish to engage in plural marriage without their consent, such as the case with the Law of Sarah.

In Doctrine and Covenants we read that Sarah gave her consent to Abraham to take Hagar as a second wife. This is the Law of Sarah; that the first wife must give her consent for her husband to take a plural wife. However, in Doctrine and Covenants we also read that if a wife does not give her consent, the law doesn't apply, "if she [the wife] receive not this law [plural marriage] . . . because she did not believe and administer unto him according to my word; and she then becomes the transgressor; and he is exempt from the law of Sarah."[16] Essentially if a wife doesn't give her consent, her husband is exempt from getting her consent—rending the Law of Sarah quite meaningless. It is also worth mentioning that there seems to be little to no concern for Hagar's consent in this narrative either.

Likewise, the Standard Model does not leave room for couples who wish to remain romantically and/or sexually monogamous. However, there is room for monogamy in the Queer Polygamy Model. To demonstrate this, I'd like to refer to queer sexual orientations, not as universal orientations or socio-political identity labels, but a specific practice in a specific relationship. For example, I identify as pansexual; however, in my relationship with my sister, I am asexual and aromantic. Though I am pansexual by orientation, I engage in a specific asexual, non-romantic relationship with her. This does not mean our relationship is void of depth, intimacy, love, commitment, and loyalty—quite the contrary. I feel all those things for my sister and more, but we have no desire for a sexual or romantic connection. This does not mean my sister is any less important to me than my husband, with whom I do desire a sexual and romantic relationship. It simply means that my relationship dynamics are different with my sister than with my husband. In the Queer Polygamy Model, I could be sealed to my sister for all eternity in the bonds of sisterhood while also being sealed to my husband in a romantic and/or sexual relationship. I would be sealed to two people plurally, but I would still be practicing sexual monogamy. Thus, for couples who desire to practice heterosexual monogamy with one partner for all eternity, they may still be sealed to other persons they love plurally and engage in those other relationships asexually and aromantically. It is in this way that we can be sealed to our children. I am not only sealed to my husband, but I'm also sealed to our three children. Not all sealings include sex, nor should they.

Plural marriages, unions, and sealings among adults could also include plural, non-sexual sealings among several persons while the core couple still practices exclusive heterosexual monogamy. For example, siblings who join the Church without their parents are not born in the covenant, and they do not share a common sealed patriarch, such as with a father. Wouldn't it make sense for the two sisters who join the Church to be able to be sealed together independent of sealing to a common patriarch? Likewise, if a father of three daughters has his membership withdrawn, formerly known as excommunication, are his three daughters still sealed together without their common patriarch? Why should their sealing to each other be contingent upon their father's standing or participation in the Church? Why not cut out the middleman and let the sisters be sealed together if they want an eternity together? The Queer Polygamy Model allows adults to be sealed in the bonds of friendship and kinship without relying on a cisgender, heterosexual, patriarchal coupling.

Second, the account given in Doctrine and Covenants 132 does not explicitly address women who also wish to engage in plural marriages alongside their husbands. The exclusively polygynous model of polygamy can create a disturbing and problematic power imbalance among genders—especially for women in heterosexual relationships. Under the Queer Polygamy Model, plural sealings would be available to all consenting adults, not just men. As stated above, women are sealed to multiple people, such as children and parents, but I suggest policy should extend to allow women to be sealed to multiple adults, just as men are afforded that privilege. The fact that the scriptures do not explicitly state that women may have more than one husband does not mean they *can't* have more than one husband. In fact, more than one of Joseph Smith's wives was also married to other men.[17] This shows there is room in our religion for women who desire to be married to multiple men, including heteroromantic, heterosexual, or asexual relationships.

It would be up to the participants to decide the relationship dynamics of their sealing or marriage, just as Joseph Smith engaged in sexual relationships with some, but not all, of his plural wives. There are various reasons for plural marriage and/or sealings that do or don't involve sex. Granted, legitimizing sexual relationships through ritual is important to avoid promiscuity. Honesty and open communication are key to respecting the autonomy and volition of all participants—though not all past participants of polygamy (notably Joseph Smith) practiced it in such a manner.

Third, a traditional interpretation of the doctrine of celestial marriage does not leave room for persons who do not desire marriage or are asexual and/or aromantic, while there is room for asexual and aromantic sealings under the Queer Polygamy Model. Sealings of kinship, friendship, and love may be offered between persons who wish not to have a sexual or romantic relationship with each other. Plural marriage for asexual persons could take the form of an asexual woman married to a heterosexual couple or three asexual persons who wish to be sealed together in a plural marriage that doesn't include sex. As demonstrated by the Law of Adoption, sealings are not tantamount to sex. The Law of Adoption could be revived to include sealings for people who want to be sealed in non-sexual or non-marital unions. Asexual persons, or persons who wish to remain single, could be sealed to parents, siblings, friends, and other partners without committing to sexualized or romanticized notions of marriage and sealings.

Fourth, the Standard Model is heteronormative and leaves out the experiences and desires for homosexual, bisexual, pansexual, and other queer persons. This may be one of the more difficult hurdles to overcome because the common perception of Latter-day Saint theology implies there is no room for homosexual unions in celestial cosmology. As demonstrated in the previous chapters, I do not see why this must necessarily be the case. Families are diverse, and creation is more expansive than biological reproduction.

The Queer Polygamy Model leaves room for same-gender and same-sex sealings, whether they are non-romantic, such as between my sister and me, or homosexual, such as between two wives. Under the Queer Polygamy model, plural marriage may include multi-gendered partnerships, such as sealings among sister-wives that may or may not allow sexual relations between them. If a man is married to two women and the women are bisexual, they may choose to be sealed to each other and have a romantic and sexual relationship with each other as well as with their common husband. Likewise, a transgender woman might be married to a cisgender man and cisgender woman, but all identify as pansexual—thus, it could be the case they are all in a romantic and sexual relationship with one another. The takeaway is that gender is irrelevant to whether or not there is sexual activity in plural sealings—assuming there is no abuse, neglect, or harm being done to the participants. The purpose of the sealing isn't to legitimatize sexual behavior; the purpose of sealings is to legitimize, reinforce, and cultivate the eternal and everlasting bonds which people share with one another, be they homosexual or otherwise.

Fifth, the Standard Model doesn't leave room for children to have the autonomy to be sealed or unsealed to diverse parents. In the Standard Model, children are property of their fathers and have little say about whether or not they may be sealed or unsealed to other parents. For example, a child born into a heterosexual marriage may be sealed to the parents, but if the father is gay, divorces his wife, and both marry other men, the child of the first marriage would have four parents—one biological father, one biological mother, and two stepfathers—but would only be sealed to the biological father and mother. Under the Queer Polygamy Model, the children could be granted plural sealings to both the biological parents and their husbands. The child would be sealed to three fathers and one mother, though the dynamics of the relationships are diverse and fluid among the parents. Essentially a child should be able to be sealed to all the parents they love. This is not the case under the Standard Model, which focuses on who the child belongs to in the eternities instead of whom the child desires to be sealed to. A child should not be forced to choose between fathers by mandates of heterosexual monogamy or patriarchal polygyny. Children with plural parents should be granted plural sealings if they want them. No child should have to divorce a parent eternally, just to be sealed to another, just as no wife should necessarily have to be unsealed to a husband to be sealed to a second. It is to the detriment of children to assume they are inherently "owned" by their biological fathers alone when children have the capacity to love more than one father and mother. Likewise, a child born to a family with three mothers and one father should have the opportunity to be sealed to all her mothers. Heaven isn't heaven without all the people we love, and if not, heaven becomes hell. I trust God feels the same.

Now that we have a broader understanding of what diverse families and sealings could look like under the Queer Polygamy Model, the words of Latter-day Saint prophets about families begin to taste sweet again. The family really is central to God's plan—it is ordained of God. We are all part of one big family—God's family. The family is far more than just one mom and dad. It is siblings, cousins, spouses, aunts, uncles, friends, grandparents, and the generations of persons who came here before you or me. The family is about creating bonds, which extend into eternity as we connect with one another to become something greater than ourselves. Family is everything, yet people often define it as something too narrow to encompass its theological bigness. It is really a grand and beautiful quilt that envelopes us all. Sealings under this broad quilt might include, but are not limited to, spouse-to-spouse sealings, parent-to-child sealings, Law of Adoption sealings, friendship sealings, and many more. Under the family quilt of Queer Polygamy, we are all interconnected in an infinite number of complex and beautiful relationships.

The spirit of polygamy is the love of community—this is the law we must embrace as Saints if we are to become Gods. The spirit of polygamy encompasses the diverse unions of the gods—in all their complexity and intricacies. The spirit of polygamy includes but also reaches beyond the legitimization of sexual relationships. The spirit of polygamy means that I might be sealed to my best friend, regardless of whether we also share a sexual relationship. It means children may be sealed to all their parents, be they biological or adoptive. It means I may be sealed to a sister wife, not *through* my husband, but *with* my husband. It means my husband may be sealed to his best friend while they enjoy an asexual, non-romantic relationship. It means that an asexual woman may choose to be sealed with a gay couple, independent of sexual activity, but still have a relationship full of meaning, emotional intimacy, and purpose. The spirit of polygamy means that heaven isn't heaven without all the people we love. It means infinite possibilities fulfilled by our infinite love—just like the gods, filled with a multiplicity of

Heavenly Mothers, Fathers, and Parents that we have yet to imagine. I cannot imagine any God more beautifully Mormon than a God of both plurality and unity who welcomes all families into Zion.

Eternity is a Long Time

Humans aren't very good at imagining eternity. I include myself in that sentiment. I suspect if we could robustly imagine eternity, we might have different ideas about plural sealings. Eternity is a long time. It is perhaps unreasonable to expect humans to imagine eternity when humans have a finite experience. As mortals, we are born, and then we die. There is a mortal beginning and end. We come up with all sorts of theories, narratives, myths, philosophies, and religions to help us grapple with our mortality. Which ones are true and which ones are false have yet to be discovered.

As Mormons, we are taught there is no beginning or end to our existence—a hypothesis that I put my faith and trust in. Knowledge is different from faith. If I had perfect knowledge of an eternal existence, I wouldn't need faith. I put faith in my hypothesis of eternity when I lack sufficient knowledge. Life is a delicate balance of living without knowledge of eternity but with hope in eternity.

When my husband and I have an argument, as many couples do, there tends to be long spaces of silence. The awkward spaces are often filled with pride, anger, hurt, bitterness, and sadness. While these spaces might be necessary for us to come back to the situation with a more constructive attitude, I do not relish our awkward silences. I'm usually the first to bend. If I'm lucky, I only get another 50 or 60 years with him on earth. I don't want to spend a single moment of that upset with the person whom I love most.

One hundred years on this planet with him is less than a blink of an eye. It's not nearly enough. It's not even a fragment of a thought in the mind of eternity. But let's say we were gifted 200 years together. Let's say my husband and I had been there the day our sixth great grandfather, Thomas Hancock II, was baptized. We would have seen our family history upfront and personal, the good and the bad, the triumphs and the mistakes. We might have met the Prophet, witnessed his martyrdom, crossed the plains, and witnessed our family's polygamous sealings. We would have seen the rise of Brigham Young, and Wilford Woodruff announcing the 1890 Manifesto. We would have seen firsthand the shift from polygamy being the ideal form of marriage to a heterosexual monogamous family being the ideal form of marriage in the Church. In 200 years, we could have seen the entire history of our religious tradition.

Yet, let's pretend radical life extension technologies gifted us 1,000 years of life together, it still would be an insignificant quantity compared to eternity, not even a footnote in the meridian of time. Even if we tripled that to 3,000 years, would that be enough? Let's be generous and say that my husband and I could live together for 5,000 years. In that time together, we would have witnessed the entirety of recorded human history. We wouldn't have just been around for the formation of the Church, Industrial Revolution, the Civil War, or the American Revolution; we would have been around for the Renaissance, the Ming Dynasty, and the rise and fall of Constantinople. We would see great empires rise and fall. We would have seen the Middle Ages, the Roman Empire, and the birth and death of Jesus. We would have walked the earth at the same time as Aristotle and Confucius. We would have seen the construction of the Great Pyramids of Giza, the Hanging Gardens of Babylon, the Lighthouse of Alexandria, the Hagia Sophia, Stonehenge, the Great Wall of China, the Taj Mahal, and Chichén Itzá.

Let's be even more generous and say we were afforded one million years together. Take a moment to pause. Try to imagine for a moment what one million years would be like with your eternal partner. Now, let's double that and make it two million years together. Creatures and species that became extinct long ago would roam the earth with us. Our home, planet Earth, might even feel alien or foreign to what we experience now. Yet, we're still not even close to approaching an eternity. Let's be even more generous and grant my husband and I two hundred and fifty million years together. That's TWO HUNDRED AND FIFTY MILLION YEARS on the planet we call Earth. We could live past the Cretaceous, Jurassic, and Triassic periods. We wouldn't only outlive the human species, but all dinosaur species as well.

Cosmologically speaking, we're still not even close to approaching what we would call "eternity." We're still only talking about millions of years together on a single planet in a single galaxy. What if we had billions of years together? Scientists estimate that our planet is about 4.5 billion years old, and our galaxy is about 13.5 billion years old. If I got the chance to live with my husband for fifty billion years, we would see the birth and death of not just our planet, our solar system, but entire galaxies. We would witness gigantic cosmological formations being swallowed up by black holes. We would see the birth of new formations after a supernova explosion. Yet, even with the gift of fifty billion years together, would we find ourselves among the Gods beginning to see time as Gods do? I doubt it. If Gods are eternal, even the vastness of the cosmos is still nothing more than a naive flirtation with the concept of eternity.

I do not believe that I nor any human is capable of imagining eternity. We live with such weak cognitive capacities that we cannot comprehend the difference between being sealed to a spouse for a measly 100 years on Earth, or a quadrillion years in the cosmos. Yet, both are nothing compared to eternity, precisely because eternity never ends.

Yet, if I'm lucky, I only get another 50 years or so on Earth with the person that I love most. As mentioned earlier, I have faith in eternity but do not have knowledge of eternity. Furthermore, even if there is such a thing as eternity, there is no guarantee eternity would be anything like what I am imagining.

What I do have knowledge of is my love for my husband and my desire to be with him. That desire is strong enough that I would do almost anything to be with him. I would bind myself to him in whatever insignificantly human way I possibly could. I would put a ring on my finger. I would construct temples, seal him to me in the holy house of the Lord and pray that this meager gesture of our love was worthy of God's consideration. I would love him in every possible way so that one day a God might be moved by our love enough to rummage through the archives of quantum archeology and breathe life into our love. Of course, such an evolved and advanced being who warrants the label "God" could perceive our union as nothing more than the random collision of atomic masses in the abyss of space. Yet, I choose faith in love, God, and eternity. I trust that gods are far more compassionate than we imagine.

Mormons are not sealed just for life. It isn't an "until death do you part" promise. When I was sealed with my husband, this was more than a gesture of a fleeting passion. It was a covenant to love him throughout all the ages of time, through this world and the next, through all epochs, and beyond. Of course, when we were seated, I didn't and still don't have any clue what an eternity with him would be like, but that doesn't stop me from wanting it. Perhaps I was a naïve 19-year-old girl dressed in the robes of the priesthood kneeling across an alter promising to give myself to a man I had only known for a year, but that description wouldn't do the moment justice. I was a person deeply in love with another person, motivated with the burning desire to express that love in a way that defied our impending mortality. Our sealing was a deliberate act of defiance of death. We had faith that our love mattered enough to be expressed through a religious ritual.

As great as the universe is, I don't feel small. I feel humbled, but also worthy. I feel love, and that matters. Even if our 100 years of love together on Earth have no more meaning than an atom on a speck of dust floating in space, I would do my best to make that atom worthy of meaning. Even if my efforts are futile and I fail miserably, I will have lived loving to the most of my abilities.

If we as Mormons take the power of eternal sealings seriously, we should not be surprised that homosexual couples and other queer folks would feel utter hopelessness at being excluded from our loved ones for eternity. Not just for one hundred years, one thousand years, one million years, one billion years, one trillion years, or even a quadrillion years, but all eternity. The denial of eternal sealings could be a fate worse than non-existence. Eternal sealings, as presently constituted, means queer folks are cut off from the people we love most. It should not be surprising that a queer person would want to die from such excruciating mental torture. I'd rather not exist than exist separated for all eternity from those whom I love most.

Yet, in the expanse of eternity, I suspect we will fall in love more than once. Who knows how many times and in what ways a god falls in love? Even in our short time on earth, falling in love happens more than once. Sometimes people talk of falling in love as if it's a one-time occurrence. If that is the case, it certainly isn't a universal experience.

Imagine a woman who lost her husband to cancer. The two of them were deeply committed and in love with one another, so much so that death did not break the bonds of their love and sealing. Long after his death, she was still in love with him. To this day, she never stopped loving him. Eventually, she fell in love again. She met a kind man who she came to care for deeply. They decided to get married in the temple. On the day of their wedding, she was still in love with her first husband. His omnipresence in her life was something she welcomed. She had no intention to stop loving him, even while she was in love with her second husband. She was in love with both her husbands. Even though one husband was dead, and one was living, she loved them both. She married both men in the temple, though due to inequitable sealing practices, she was only sealed to the first husband. If she had been a man with two wives, she could have been sealed to both spouses, assuming the woman was not sealed to another man. Sadly, according to current Latter-day Saint policy, she will have to wait until her own death to be sealed to both husbands via proxy.

When I consider her situation, I wonder what happens when death no longer separates spouses. In the resurrection, will she be forced to choose between her husbands? One might assume so on account of her being a woman, but if men are not forced to choose between wives, why must a woman be forced to choose between husbands? Why must a woman live in eternal monogamy while a man may choose plurality? If spouses are forced to let go of each other for all eternity, I imagine the resurrection day will be a day of great mourning—when husbands and wives are decoupled, disconnected, ripped from each other's arms, and tortured because we refused to see love as something plural or queer. As Emily Dickenson once wrote in her poem, parting is all we need of hell.[18]

> My life closed twice before its close—
> It yet remains to see
> If Immortality unveil
> A third event to me
>
> So huge, so hopeless to conceive
> As these that twice befell.
> Parting is all we know of heaven,
> And all we need of hell.

In an existence where death no longer parts people, the real hell would be separating from those we love most on account of prejudice. This is not just a temporary separation, but a separation for all eternity. I'm not so sure such a hell would be bearable. Eternal non-existence might be preferable. I imagine more than one queer person has contemplated the hell of eternal banishment.

Of course, there are and will be people who wish to have an eternity of monogamy, and by no means is it my place to tell them otherwise. Yet, as equally important, it is not their place to tell others to limit their love to one person of the opposite gender for all eternity.

In my short 37 years of life on earth, I have fallen in love more than once. I was even in love with another man when I knelt across the altar and married my husband. In a world where love is limited to two, three is perceived as misbehaving. However, I don't think loving more than two people at the same time is a sin or immoral by any stretch of the imagination. Love isn't a sin. Of course, the ways we express our love for one another should be thoughtful and cautious. We don't always get to love people in the ways we want to love them. I don't claim all desires should be acted upon, even loving desires, but loving someone is never a sin.[19] Loving another soul is perhaps the godliest thing we do.[20] The tragedy is not loving more than one person. The tragedy is demanding that someone must die for me to be granted social allowance to express my love for more than one spouse. My husband shouldn't have to die for it to be morally or socially acceptable to express my love for another or be sealed to another in a holy temple.

I imagine gods love in ways that defy convention and mortality. When death becomes the legitimizing force for plural love, what happens when we are no longer bound by death? What happens when we are alive for all eternity? Do we honestly believe that immortal Gods who live for all eternity will not desire or be capable of loving more than one fellow God? In this thought experiment, I imagine there would be many different relationships among Gods. Some may wish to remain single, some monogamous, and some polygamous. The problem is not monogamy or plurality. The problem is demanding sameness among the Gods, or thinking that we are even capable of understanding the eternities as They do.

My husband wasn't the first person I fell in love with. He's also not the last person I fell in love with. I suspect there will be much more falling in love throughout the eternities. When I imagine eternity with him, not just 100 years, 1,000 years, 100,000 years, or 1,000,000,000 years, but all eternity with him, I do not think that falling in love is something that could or should be contained to us. I may never get the chance to be sealed to all the people I love, but then again, eternity is a long time.

CHAPTER 7

Concerning Policy

The thesis of this book is to demonstrate how Mormon theology is inherently queer. If this is true—and evidence abounds that it is—then our policies should reflect our theology. Granted, this depends on how we interpret our theology. There are many interpretations that do not share my optimism for queer inclusion. In this section, I address and critique such interpretations in favor of a theology that supports autonomy, inclusivity, and liberation from rigid gender assignments..

I remain quite hopeful that our policies can root out prejudice to create a more Christ-centered experience for all Latter-day Saints. As stated in the *General Handbook*, "Prejudice is not consistent with the revealed word of God." Not only is prejudice inconsistent with the word of God, but we are also called to do something about it.

> The Church calls on all people to abandon attitudes and actions of prejudice toward any group or individual. Members of the Church should lead out in promoting respect for all of God's children. Members follow the Savior's commandment to love others. They strive to be persons of goodwill toward all, rejecting prejudice of any kind. This includes prejudice based on race, ethnicity, nationality,

tribe, gender, age, disability, socioeconomic status, religious belief or nonbelief, and sexual orientation.[1]

I hope all Latter-day Saints take this sentiment seriously and consider exactly what they can do to abandon attitudes of prejudice on account of "race, ethnicity, nationality, tribe, gender, age, disability, socioeconomic status, religious belief or nonbelief, and sexual orientation." I recognize that the average member of the Church doesn't have significant influence over policies like ordination, baptisms, and sealings. However, there are things that each of us can do to promote an environment of inclusivity. I close this section with a list of 15 things members and leaders can do right now to make the Church a safer place for queer folks as we reject prejudice that is not in line with the revealed word of God.

Priesthood Ordination

Is there something inherently masculine about the priesthood that makes women unfit or unworthy to be ordained to act in the name of God? It may seem that way according to current policy. In the androcentric interpretation of Mormon theology, God is a Heavenly Father, who put men in charge of His church, and those men tell us that God wants only cisgender men to be ordained to His priesthood. In this reductive interpretation of our theology, Heavenly Father becomes a tyrant who implicitly teaches that maleness is next to godliness. If that is the case, there is little a woman can do about her gender assignment to increase in her "godliness," as transgender men are also denied priesthood ordination.

If the priesthood is about masculinity and maleness, then surely those men who were assigned female at birth should have the privilege of priesthood ordination too. But alas, they too are prohibited from ordination, along with cisgender women. Not only that, but transgender men might also even be formally disciplined or have their membership withdrawn. Therefore, priesthood ordination is a privilege of assignment, not a privilege of desire or merit. In this model, a cisgender woman seeking ordination is implicitly unworthy to be ordained on account of her sex. Regardless of her commitment, works, performance, ability, desire, or intellect, she is barred from ordination. The rejection of transgender men from priesthood ordination implicitly tells cisgender women who desire ordination that their gender is a sin they can never repent of.

It is nonsensical to teach cisgender women that they are supposed to be like Heavenly Father while simultaneously telling them that, if they change their gender, they become less godly. It makes little sense to give a cisgender woman a prominent male role model to aspire toward and then condemn her for aspiring toward that goal. If she is not supposed to adopt Heavenly Father's godly attributes, she should at least have a clear and equally prominent Heavenly Mother to aspire toward.[2] Unfortunately, the masculine side of God has overshadowed the feminine side of God in our culture, music, worship, art, and ritual.

However, if we look back to the second chapter of this book at the description of God as both male and female, we can see that God is not "He" or "She" in any exclusive sense, but rather "They." If God is both "He" and "She" combined in a cooperative union, maleness is no closer to godliness than femaleness. Both are necessary to the composition of godhood—whether it is seen in intersex or non-binary persons, a heterosexual transgender marriage, or the alliance of men and women cooperating together—the composition of God includes men and women working creatively together. We are all made in the image of God, and all genders ought to have the privilege of priesthood ordination according to their faith and works, rather than by virtue of an assignment predicated primarily on their genitalia.

Even though I desire ordination for all genders, I do not conflate priesthood power solely with patriarchal church governance.[3] That would be a narrow interpretation of the full scope of priesthood power. I believe it is possible to approach priesthood power with more equity as exemplified by Jesus, and ordination is only one aspect of that. The important questions here are, what is priesthood power, and why should anyone want it?

Priesthood power is how we gain knowledge of God, the power by which the universe is governed, and is the authority to act in the name of God. The priesthood "administereth the gospel and holdeth the key of the mysteries of the kingdom, even the key of the knowledge of God."[4] We cannot know God without priesthood power. John Taylor stated that the priesthood "governs all things—it directs all things—it sustains all things—and has to do with all things that God and truth are associated with. It is the Power of God delegated to intelligences in the heaven . . . and on the earth."[5] John A. Widtsoe said, "Priesthood implies purpose. The purpose of the Plan, made clear in modern revelation, is the eternal, progressive welfare of human beings."[6] In short, priesthood power is God's work and knowledge, and that work is stated in scripture, "For behold, this is my work and my glory to bring to pass the immortality and eternal life of man."[7] I'm confident that includes women too.

We read in the Book of Mormon that those who are ordained to take upon them the high priesthood, becoming high priests forever after the order of Jesus Christ "who is full of grace, equity, and truth."[8] Note the word "equity" is used to describe our earthly exemplar for priesthood power. If God's priesthood power is exemplified through Jesus Christ, there should be equal opportunity for participation through ordination, as we have all been invited to be one in Christ. As stated in Corinthians, "Now ye are the body of Christ, and members in particular."[9]

Priesthood represents a godly power worth seeking after and magnifying. Indeed, Joseph Smith taught that we should seek after the mysteries of godliness. "I advise all to go on in perfection and search deeper and deeper into the mysteries of godliness."[10] Seeking after ordination is not in opposition to, but an expression of faith in priesthood power.

The desire for ordination can also be seen in the example of Abraham, who specifically sought out priesthood power.[11] We read:

> And finding there was greater happiness and peace and rest for me, I sought for the blessings of the fathers, and the right whereinto I should be ordained to administer the same; having been myself a follower of righteousness, desiring also to be one who possessed greater knowledge, and righteousness, and to possess a greater knowledge, and to be a father of many nations, a prince of peace, and desiring to receive instructions, and to keep the commandments of God, I became a rightful heir, a High Priest, holding the right belonging to the fathers.[12]

Abraham "desired to be ordained" to "possess greater knowledge and righteousness." As a "follower of righteousness," he "became a rightful heir, a High Priest." Women and queer folks who seek ordination for further knowledge and righteousness are not so different from Abraham, for whom ordination was a reward for his righteous desires.

Of course, one key difference between Abraham and myself is that I am a queer woman, and Abraham was a man. Some claim that a woman's desire for ordination is tantamount to "vying for authority" that is not hers. Yet, if a man desires ordination, he is fulfilling his divine duty. Her authentic desire is greeted with skepticism and condemnation, yet a man's desire is greeted with enthusiasm and confirmation—not simply *conformation*, but literal *confirmation*. His desire will be upheld, protected, nursed, and celebrated. Hers has been ridiculed, rejected, shamed, and condemned. Could I ever be embraced with the same authenticity as Abraham? The answer to that question isn't entirely up to me.

I remember one conversation with an ordained priesthood holder. When I apprehensively opened up to him and told him about my desire to be ordained, his response left me in tears. He told me, "If you really want to be ordained to the priesthood, you're better off starting your own sect of Mormonism. Maybe the Church isn't for you." I remember getting in my car after the brief conversation uselessly trying to fight back the tears. This was not the first time I was told I didn't belong in my own church, but this was the first time I took it seriously.

Maybe Elder Uchtdorf was wrong. Maybe there isn't room for me in this church. It didn't matter how much I believed in priesthood power independent of ordination; all that mattered was that my gender assignment didn't match the job description. Why would any loving God create a requirement that would neglect half their children? Was my desire ungodly? Or was my gender ungodly? Had I been assigned "male," I could be ordained. Perhaps what was most ungodly according to the stewards of tradition was the rejection of my assignment. After all, a trans woman is also considered ungodly for the same reason. She rejected her assignment in favor of personal revelation, and for this reason, she is my comrade.

We are experiencing the tangible consequences of the belief that God is exclusively or principally male, which is a reductive interpretation of our own, inherently expansive theology. If God is exclusively a man, we are living in the imagination of men, or man's mind, that has fashioned a God in man's image at the expense of other genders.

Yet, according to Mormon theology, God is more than a man. God is a creator, and God's power is the power to enable all life. God is life. God's priesthood power is the power to enable life and flourishing, and anyone who desires to share in these priesthood goals should be celebrated and welcomed through ordination. If the priesthood is the power and authority to act in the name of God—to participate in the work of creation, organization, immortality, and resurrection— I can find no fault in a person's desire to be more fully involved in priesthood responsibilities and religious rituals that motivate us toward these godly goals. Any gender should be eligible for God's ordained power.

The Exclusion Policy

On November 3, 2015, a new section in the *Church Handbook of Instructions* was released. The new section excluded the children of homosexual parents from receiving a baby blessing, baptism, confirmation, ordination for males, or serving as a missionary unless the child disavows their parents' homosexuality.[13] Adaptations were also made in section 6.7.3 that deemed same-gender marriage an act of apostasy, which warranted a mandatory disciplinary council.[14]

It would be difficult to overstate the outcry among Latter-day Saints in the days that followed. There was communal anguish, as queer Latter-day Saints and allies grappled with these changes. I was one of them. My son was scheduled to be baptized when the policy was released. In the early stages of mourning, I wrote in my journal:

> I just finished crying when Preston and William came into my room this morning at 6:07 am. Preston asked, "Mom, why are you frowning?"
>
> "Our church did something very sad. They are making it very difficult for a certain group of children to get baptized among other things. It's upsetting when the leadership of The Church of Jesus Christ of Latter-day Saints does things that make it difficult for people to be like Jesus Christ. They shouldn't make it difficult for children to get baptized."
>
> William interjected, "Even if they are 8 years old!? Why would they do that?"
>
> I continued, "Remember how we talked about different types of families? Some families have two mommies. Some have two daddies. Some have only one mommy and no daddy. Some have a daddy and no mommy. Some have lots of mommies. There are many different

types of families. The children that come from families that don't look like ours are being treated poorly. They didn't do anything wrong. It's just sheer silliness."

Preston responded, "No, it isn't silliness. It's a disaster!"

William hugged me, "Mom, why are you wet? Are those your tears?"

"Yes. It's a thing mommies do sometimes. We just love our children so much that when other people's children are hurt, we cry for their children too."

I cried many tears as my husband and I debated over whether or not to continue with our son's scheduled baptism. We were also uncertain as to whether he would be eligible or not. As a bisexual woman in a heterosexual marriage, it wasn't entirely clear whether or not my son would qualify for baptism under this new policy.

Ten days after the first announcement, a statement was issued by The First Presidency clarifying the changes to the Handbook. They reaffirmed their position that same-gender marriage warranted church discipline. They also clarified that the policy only applied to children whose primary residence included a parent in a homosexual relationship. Identifying as gay, lesbian, or bisexual did not warrant disciplinary action, nor would their children be subject to the Exclusion Policy. Children of parents in a homosexual relationship who were already baptized, ordained, or serving a mission would not have their privileges revoked.[15]

Even though my son could still be baptized, I was torn between being queer and a Latter-day Saint. My son was spared from the policy, but other children were not. Up to that point, I had been content not to be public about being bisexual, but after the Exclusion Policy, my silence felt complicit. Why should my child be spared, but the children of my queer peers be sacrificed? Aren't all children alike and blameless in the eyes of God?

Some might question the authenticity or rationality of my suffering since my children were not direct targets of the Exclusion Policy. It's true that if I wanted to use my heterosexual passing privilege, I could have my children baptized. Yet this use of privilege would be the opposite of what Jesus taught. Jesus took on the responsibilities and pains of the world through the atonement. He made our suffering His suffering. There was no *Him* or *me*. In Gethsemane, we were *us*. Through the atonement, we became *us*. To wash my hands of accountability while innocent children suffered would be to take on the role of Pilate. I saw their suffering, and it became my suffering. There was no difference between their children and my children. They became *our* children as we took on the shape of each other's pain.

Some tried to justify this policy as a product of love, but it didn't feel like a loving policy to most of the queer families who were affected by it. Others contended that, despite the policy, nothing would be lost with these children because they could choose to participate in saving ordinances in adulthood.[16] However, if the children were able to accept saving ordinances at a later time, then why does it matter if any children participate in these ordinances? If "nothing is lost," then why participate at all when we could just wait until we die and have our ordinances done by proxy? We have been warned not to procrastinate the day of our salvation, yet this policy encouraged the procrastination of saving ordinances.[17]

The truth is that these children did experience loss. They were denied community, participation, ritual, baptism, and confirmation. They experienced the shunning of a once-beloved and cherished religious community. As for their parents, I don't imagine I'm the only one that experienced the traumatizing heartbreak of rejection.

Surprisingly, three and half years later, on April 4, 2019, The First Presidency released a statement during the leadership session of General Conference. Elder Dallin H. Oaks shared that the Exclusion Policy would be revoked. In addition, same-gender marriage would no longer be treated as an act of apostasy but as a serious transgression. The official announcement released by the First Presidency stated,

> At the direction of The First Presidency, President Oaks shared that effective immediately, children of parents who identify themselves as lesbian, gay, bisexual or transgender may be baptized without First Presidency approval if the custodial parents give permission for the baptism and understand both the doctrine that a baptized child will be taught and the covenants he or she will be expected to make.[18]

Though the policy reversal did not come with an apology to the persons, families, and children deeply affected by the Exclusion Policy, this was very good news. Children of queer parents, regardless of their marital or relationship status, could be baptized and confirmed members of the Church if it was their desire.

The reversal of the Exclusion Policy is a testament to the gift of continuing revelation, which is not a task reserved for an elite group of individuals. Continuing revelation is an ongoing process implemented by all who are seeking improvement. Continuing revelation is the percolation of powerful ideas through a robust network of individuals and influences. Latter-day Saints embody revelation when we weep, speak, act, and bear witness. I have no doubt that the efforts, letters, and actions of concerned Latter-day Saints on behalf of queer families contributed to the policy reversal. I trust there are many more beautiful revelations on the horizon if we move forward with love as our compass.

Celestial Conversion Therapy

Conversion therapy, also called "reparative therapy" or "aversion therapy," is the pseudo-scientific practice of trying to change a person's sexual orientation or gender identity. Conversion therapy techniques include, but are not limited to: chemical castration, hormonal injections, icepick lobotomies, electroshocks on the genitals, nausea-inducing drugs during homoerotic stimulation, and masturbatory reconditioning.[19] Some have even resorted to transplanting the testicles of straight men into gay men in an attempt to change their sexual orientation.[20] While these practices have been generally abandoned, modern forms of conversion therapy include, but are not limited to: psychoanalytic therapy, pornographic visualizations, verbal abuse, and spiritual interventions.[21] Current research shows that not only are these treatments ineffective, they are harmful, with many recipients reporting an increase in depression, anxiety, suicide ideation, and suicidality.[22]

In recent years, many medical and mental health professionals, associations, and organizations have come out against the practice of conversion therapy. The American Academy of Pediatrics stated, "Therapy directed at specifically changing sexual orientation is contraindicated since it can provoke guilt and anxiety while having little or no potential for achieving changes in orientation."[23] The American College of Physicians opposes the use of "conversion," "reorientation," or "reparative" therapy for the treatment of queer folks, and The American Psychological Association literature review found that reparative therapy is associated with the "loss of sexual feeling, depression, anxiety, and suicidality."[24] The American Medical Association abandoned the practice in 1996, then voiced opposition to it in 2012.[25] The American Psychiatric Association, the American Psychoanalytic Association, and the American Psychological Association have all abandoned the harmful practice of conversion therapy.[26] All have cited conversion therapy as increasing the risk of depression, anxiety, and suicidality. Fifteen states already have bans on conversion therapy on minors, and more are following suit.[27] The Church of Jesus Christ of Latter-day Saints has also denounced the harmful practice of conversion therapy, stating that, "Research demonstrates that electric shock, aversion and other analogous therapies are ineffective and harmful to youth who experience same-sex attraction."[28]

I applaud these organizations for condemning the harmful practice of conversion therapy, especially the Church. Even though the Church previously participated in conversion therapies on queer Latter-Day Saints, they have since denounced the practice as harmful.[29] It wasn't long ago that Spencer W. Kimball lamented the fact that the death penalty could not be used on homosexuals.[30] Considering that clergymen once advocated for conversion therapy and even the death of queer Latter-day Saints, it is laudable to see such a significant improvement in church policy. I applaud the many faithful Latter-day Saints who petitioned for further light and knowledge concerning the health and safety of queer Latter-day Saints. This is truly remarkable.

Though the Church has condemned conversion therapy as a harmful practice, conversion therapy folk theologies still persist in the Latter-day Saint imagination. Some Latter-day Saints profess that queer Latter-day Saints will no longer be queer in the next life and be "cured" of their gender deviant desires. This folk theology seems to have started in 2006 with Lance Wickman, a member of the Seventy. In an interview with LDS Public Affairs, he stated that "Same-gender attraction did not exist in the pre-earth life and neither will it exist in the next life."[31] Wickman also compared queerness to a temporary disability that would be fixed after death.

Theological interpretations that advocate for queer persons being "fixed" before entering heaven are tantamount to "Celestial Conversion Therapy," or more accurately put, "Queer Celestial Genocide." Suggesting queer folks will be turned into cisgender, heterosexuals in the next life assumes celestial beings are not queer beings. Essentially, a queer person simply could not exist in the presence of God.

Imagine if the roles were reversed and celestial narratives were controlled by queer supremacists imposing celestial conversion therapy on cisgender heterosexuals. Pretend we talked to them the way that they talk to us. We would tell them that we needed to "fix" them because we love them. We would tell them a queer God will take away their heterosexual, cisgender desires and make them, well, queer.

Despite the Church speaking out against the harmful practice of conversion therapy, there are still Latter-day Saints who suggest conversion therapy will cure queer folks in the next life. You haven't stopped the harmful practice of conversion therapy; you've simply postponed it. If queer people will be "fixed" upon mortal death, mortal death becomes the quickest path to end our pain. However, you misunderstand me if you think the pain ends with the physical death of a queer mortal body. No. In this harmful folk theology, our pain will not end upon our mortal death. The pain only ends upon our spiritual death—when our community transforms our souls and bodies into cisgender, heterosexual drones. At this point, we will truly no longer exist. Celestial glory controlled by straight supremacists is the celestial genocide of queer bodies and spirits.

To reflect the Church's statement that conversion therapy is harmful, we need to stop spreading folk theologies that suggest queer Latter-day Saints will be "fixed," "cured," or "repaired" in the afterlife. Persisting in this harmful folk theology is a failure to believe what the Church has stated about conversion therapy is true. Conversion therapy is harmful and ineffective. If conversion therapy is harmful on earth, it's harmful in heaven too. Postponing it until heaven is not the kind gesture some seem to think it is. Not only that, but celestial conversion therapy also puts queer Latter-day Saints in the position of dreading celestial glory when celestial glory means queer extinction. If the Church recognizes the harms of conversion therapy enough to change policy, it makes sense that our theology would support this new revelation.

Marriage, Sealings, and Commitment

Latter-day Saints value commitment and loyalty, especially through marriage. Marriage is highly encouraged in the Mormon tradition and is required for the highest degree of celestial glory.[32] Commitment through temple sealings is supremely important. Whatever is bound on earth will be bound eternally in the heavens.[33] For believers, commitment, marriage, and loyalty are heavenly, not merely earthly endeavors. *The Family: A Proclamation to the World* states, ". . . the divine plan of happiness enables family relationships to be perpetuated beyond the grave. Sacred ordinances and covenants available in holy temples make it possible for individuals to return to the presence of God and for families to þe united eternally."[34]

Jesus taught that a couple who are committed to each other "is no more twain, but one flesh," and whatever God has joined, let no one put asunder.[35] Dishonesty and betrayal of your partners' loyalty are offenses not taken lightly.[36] Jesus even warned that we should not abandon our spouse(s) without sufficient reason.[37]

Loyalty and commitment extend beyond spouses to children. Those who abandon their spouses and children commit a serious offense. There is even a temple recommend question that asks, "Do you have financial or other obligations to a former spouse or children? If yes, are you currently meeting those obligations?"[38] People who do not fulfill their parental commitments and responsibilities are not eligible for a temple recommend.

Furthermore, through baptism, Latter-day Saints promise to take upon ourselves the name of Christ. When we take the sacrament each Sunday, we renew this covenant.[39] In temples, we also make covenants that bind us to each other, not just for time but all eternity. The importance of eternal commitment in Mormon doctrine cannot be overstated.

Accessibility to eternal sealings is important. By denying same-sex, plural, or queer couples the ability to enter into temple marriages and sealings, we undermine the value of eternal sealings by cutting off people on account of gender preferences. And when queer folks are excluded from full participation and rejected from churches, temples, communities, homes, and families, we shouldn't be surprised when they engage in risky, promiscuous, or harmful behaviors. As members of the community, we have cut off their access to healthy, loving, committed, stable relationships and then wonder why they are engaging in reckless sexual behavior. We didn't give queer folks a lot of options other than permanent celibacy or having sex with a spouse you aren't sexually attracted to.

If we, as Mormons, genuinely believe that eternal marriages, sealings, and commitments are essential to God's plan, if we genuinely believe that people in committed relationships are essential to building healthy societies, if we genuinely believe sex should be within the bounds of marriage, we should celebrate all marriages and unions made among consenting adults. Both plural marriage and gay marriage should be enthusiastically welcomed by Latter-day Saints as a symbol of commitment to the doctrine of eternal marriage. Furthermore, we should encourage married people to live up to those covenants. If not, we mistakenly contribute to the very problems that we claim to be avoiding. If people want to be committed to each other, by all means, let's seal them and help them be committed to each other, not just for time, but all eternity.

Morality Beyond Gender

I suggest we adopt a better model of determining whether a relationship is moral or not. The model provided in this section is predicated on four important concepts in Mormon theology: (1) love, (2) joy, (3) life, and (4) agency. This model accounts for diverse genders and sexual orientations, including fixed and fluid identities, but it definitely does not insist that "anything goes." I propose to use the five concepts of theology to assess the morality of a relationship through scripture, tradition, reason, experience, and the Spirit. I propose we adopt a model that will maximize life and flourishing while also accounting for diverse desires.

First, God gave us the two Great Commandments through Jesus Christ. That commandment is to love God and love each other. The scriptures explicitly state no other command can conflict with the first: "One these two commandments hang all the law on the prophets."[40] If a prophet is giving a command that conflicts with the greatest law of love, they are not speaking as a prophet. Our relationships must be predicated first and foremost on love.

Second, in the scriptures, we are taught that we exist that we might have joy.[41] Happiness is essential in God's plan. In fact, Latter-day Saints even have a name for it. It's called the "Great Plan of Happiness." Our relationships with one another should reflect the teaching that our Heavenly Parents want their children to be happy and joyful.

Third, we are also taught that God's purposes are also our purposes. As baptized Latter-day Saints, we commit to taking on the role of Christ every time we take the sacrament. We are also taught in Moses that God's purpose is to bring to pass the immortality and eternal life of all human beings.[42] Not only that, but this is also God's glory. Life is essential to "The Plan of Happiness." Our relationships should encourage the flourishing of life.

Fourth, according to scripture, we must respect agency. Lucifer became Satan because he sought to take away our agency and compel us to be obedient in all things.[43] Reason also tells us that agency and consent are interlinked. If we do not respect the consent of each other, we are not respecting their agency. Furthermore, if a person or child is in a position where their ability to give meaningful consent is compromised, we should protect them until they are able to give meaningful consent. Our relationships should respect the participant's agency and their ability to give meaningful consent.

With these four tenets taken from the Mormon tradition, we now have a structural model to help us determine if a relationship is moral or not. In this model, we should ask ourselves (1) Does this relationship promote love? (2) Does this relationship promote joy? (3) Does this relationship promote life? (4) Does this relationship respect agency and meaningful consent? These are the questions we should be focusing on. When we do, we will find that there are plenty of heterosexual relationships that are immoral and plenty of homosexual relationships that are moral. Morality is not determined by whether I was "Born That Way" or if my gender conforms to cisnormative expectations. It is determined by love, joy, life, and agency.

Furthermore, if we use this criterion to measure the morality of a gender expression, we will find that there are cisgender expressions of gender that are immoral and transgender expressions of gender that are moral. For example, if a cisgender man expresses his gender or masculinity by violently hitting his children and wife, we can conclude this is an immoral gender expression that does not promote the tenants of love, joy, life, and agency. However, the gender expression of a transgender woman who is relieved of her gender dysphoria by taking hormones is morally consistent with the ideas of love, joy, life, and agency.

In conclusion, we can see that neither queerness nor straightness is not what determines morality. All genders and sexual orientations can engage in moral or immoral behaviors. Whether they are "Born That Way" is irrelevant. The concern isn't if you were "Born That Way" or "Became That Way," the concern is if you are engaging in behaviors that provoke and inspire you toward your godly potential.

15 Ways to be More Inclusive

Even though we may not have any significant influence over changing the aforementioned policies, there are still things we can do right now to be more inclusive and to improve the experience of women and queer folks within the Church.

A dear friend of mine was recently called to her Stake Young Women presidency. She asked for my suggestions on how she and other leaders could be more inclusive of young women and queer youth. With the help of some of my peers and friends, I compiled a list of practical ways Latter-day Saint leaders can be more inclusive. Even if you don't have a calling with a lot of influence on policy, please consider how you can help in whatever capacity you can.

1. Educate Yourself on the Latest Developments

Go to MormonandGay.lds.org and learn more about the latest teachings from the Church. Dallin H. Oaks stated, "What is changing—and what needs to change—is to help Church members respond sensitively and thoughtfully when they encounter same-sex attraction in their own families, among other church members or elsewhere." [44]

2. Create Space for Honest Discussion

Make spaces for honest discussions in which young women and queer youth can share their unique experiences and testimonies without negative backlash. Include nuance and understanding that everyone is different and that we don't always have to think or testify the same way. Allow them to share their feelings, struggles, questions, and concerns without immediately correcting or stifling them. Validate their existence as a child of God by affirming their authentic experiences. Be willing to listen to the youth; they have genuine and important experiences to share.

3. Say Heavenly Parents

Say Heavenly Parents as much as possible. It is one of the most authentically Mormon ways to include Heavenly Mother and other projections of God. The ultimate goal of Mormon theology is to become our Heavenly Parents. By leaving the trajectory open to diverse experiences, genders, identities, and family structures, Young Women and queer youth can more fully see that they too are made in the image of God and that eternal families are diverse.

4. Acknowledge Queer Youth

Queer people are certainly a part of our congregations, whether we know it or not. We should speak about queer folks as if we are present because we are. A simple acknowledgment can mean the world to a queer youth. As stated by Elder L. Whitney Clayton,

> I now speak directly to Church members who experience same-sex attraction or who identify as gay, lesbian or bisexual. We want you to know we love you. You are welcome. We want you to be part of our congregations. You have great talents and abilities to offer God's kingdom on earth, and we recognize the many valuable contributions you make.[45]

For me, this was the first time I ever heard a church leader even say the word "bisexual," and I'm 37 years old. I cannot explain how much it meant to me to hear the word "bisexual" come out of the mouth of a church leader. It felt like I existed. Not only that, but I was also being told I was wanted in the congregation. Sure, it doesn't always feel that way every Sunday but saying it is a good start.

•

5. Talk about Women and the Priesthood

Talk about women and the priesthood. Don't shy away from it. Talk about the differences between priesthood power and ordination. Just because a woman isn't ordained doesn't mean she can't invoke and embody priesthood power. Talk about the priesthood responsibilities of women in the temple, such as washing and anointing rituals and women donning the robes of the Aaronic and Melchizedek priesthood. Talk about priesthood responsibilities and rituals of women in early Church history, including blessings of healing, midwife blessings, blessing by the laying on of hands with oil, and blessing animals. Talk about the historical origins and structure of the Relief Society. Talk about how Joseph Smith was recorded saying that he "turned the keys" over to the Society and that he would make this Society a "kingdom of priests."[46] Prepare and educate the young women for ordination if or when that day arrives. If the revelation comes, they should be ready.

6. Include Queer Adults

Include as many queer Latter-day Saint adults as possible in this effort. If queer youth don't see queer adults at church, they won't see a future trajectory for themselves in the Church—there's no pattern to follow. Ask queer Latter-day Saint adults to pray and speak. Give them callings and responsibilities. This also includes allowing queer adults to express themselves and their faith as genuinely as possible. We need honest stories and testimonies from queer folks. Present queer adults as a shining example. Don't fear them. If queer youth can't see a hopeful future to aspire to, suicide can become an appealing option. I know this can be intimidating and difficult when feelings have been hurt, and lives have been traumatized. We are all exploring new territory, and we must love and trust one another as we mend bridges together.

7. Host a Fireside

Host a special fireside on women and the priesthood. Invite women to speak who are well-versed in matters of early Church history and contemporary priesthood practices and policies. Consider assigning the young women priesthood topics and have them research past and present priesthood responsibilities, rituals, and practices. Follow the guidance of President Russell M. Nelson, who said, "My dear sisters, whatever your calling, whatever your circumstances, we need your impressions, your insights, and your inspiration. We need you to speak up and speak out in ward and stake councils."[47]

8. Include Women Speakers in the High Council Circuit

Include women stake leaders in the speaking circuit with high councilmen. It's an easy way to show that women can speak from a pulpit with communal authority even if they are not on the high council. If possible, call queer folks to stake callings so they can be included in the speaking circuit as well. If you are already doing this, fantastic!

9. Combine Activities

Combine as many activities as possible. Integrate the sexes beyond heteronormative assumptions about orientation and attraction. Growing up bisexual, it felt very odd that people assumed we should cater to heteronormative assumptions about sexual attraction. It felt like we were purposefully segregated to avoid sexual tension, but if that were really the case, bisexuals would need to be isolated, quarantined, and segregated from all people because we can be sexually attracted to anyone. It was a harsh message to hear in my youth because people acted as if my sexuality were something that isolated me from all genders, not just males.

Also, for many youth who are transgender, intersex, or non-binary, attending sex-segregated meetings is difficult. Many wards do a combined activity once a month. These activities can be a way to include youth in your ward who don't identify with their assigned gender. Reaching out to such youth and specifically inviting them to combined activities is an easy way to include them in ward activities without gender segregation.

10. Respect Gender Identity

Respect a person's gender identity. If a youth asks you to use different pronouns, respect their request. Likewise, respect their gender expression. If a transgender boy wants to wear a shirt and tie to a Young Women's meeting, let them. There is nothing in the handbook that says they can't, and it costs you nothing.

11. Teach That Women Are More Than Mothers

Teach women that they are valuable for reasons that go beyond motherhood. Encourage their other interests and accomplishments. Give them options to aspire to that may or may not include motherhood. Try encouraging parenthood as a balanced option with a partner, as opposed to motherhood being their only source of worth and value in the community.

In Young Women, I was implicitly and explicitly taught that my worth as a woman was tied to my ability to produce children. This caused a lot of damage because I was born with an abnormal uterus (among other issues) and was uncertain about how or if I could have children. Looking back, I repeatedly put my life on the line during pregnancy to prove my worth as a woman. Sisters who cannot or do not wish to have children often feel like they don't belong at church. Women have many talents, gifts, and abilities that may or may not include motherhood.

12. Hold Special Workshops

Hold special workshops addressing the needs of queer youth. Allow them to speak if they feel so inclined. Allow them the opportunity to talk about their concerns, fears, and troubles. Let them ask hard questions about queer issues. Hold workshops to educate adult ward and stake members. From my experience, some of the greatest challenges are coming from the adults and older generations, not the youth. Invite queer adults to speak about their experiences. Ask them to share their testimonies and how they have integrated the Gospel into their lives. Ask queer adults educated in queer issues to speak and set the example of how queer adults can have authentic testimonies focusing on love, compassion, and charity.

13. Stay Humble

There is so much we don't know. The restoration is still happening. Don't pretend to have all the answers. Saying "I don't know" is one way to show epistemic humility while leaving the door open for continuing revelation.

14. Let Them Go

Queer kids need to know that in this current climate, it is okay not to be at church. They may experience a better spiritual life in an environment that doesn't condemn their orientation or gender experience. They need to know there is happiness outside of the Church. It is reasonable for them to leave the Church for the sake of their mental health and safety, especially when many suffer from self-harm or suicidal thoughts. If they can't see a future for themselves in the Church, a future outside the Church is better than no future at all.

Additionally, it is important for leaders and other youth to demonstrate that their friendships are not contingent on church attendance. They need to know they have a friendship whether they choose to stay or go. If you love them, sometimes it's okay to let them go. According to Elder Quentin L. Cook, Latter-day Saints should be at the forefront of love and compassion. He states that we need to be a part of the family circle, which also implies the ward and stake family circle.

> As a church, nobody should be more loving and compassionate. No family who has anybody who has same-gender issues should exclude them from the family circle. They need to be part of the family circle . . . let us be at the forefront in terms of expressing love, compassion, and outreach to those and let's not have families exclude or be disrespectful of those who choose a different lifestyle as a result of their feelings about their own gender . . . I feel very strongly about this . . . It's a very important principle.[48]

15. Love Them

Love them. Love them. Love them. Teach love, charity, and compassion, and then live it. Elder Dieter F. Uchtdorf stated:

> "To put it simply, having charity and caring for one another is not simply a good idea. It is not simply one more item in a seemingly infinite list of things we ought to consider doing. It is at the core of the gospel—an indispensable, essential, foundational element. Without this transformational work of caring for our fellowmen,

the Church is but a facade of the organization God intends for His people. Without charity and compassion, we are a mere shadow of who we are meant to be—both as individuals and as a church. Without charity and compassion, we are neglecting our heritage and endangering our promise as children of God. No matter the outward appearance of our righteousness, if we look the other way when others are suffering, we cannot be justified."[49]

Jesus Christ taught that the first and great commandment is to love God and the second is to love others as thyself. On these two commandments hang all the law and prophets. The scriptures teach that we will be known as true disciples of Christ if we love one another. And there is no fear in love. We cannot know God if we do not know love, for God is love.

AFTERWORD

Concerning the Beehive

The cover of this book features a rainbow beehive. This symbol represents far more than a trendy queer take on Mormon history and culture. The rainbow beehive is an unofficial queer Mormon coat of arms.

Since the origins of Mormonism, early pioneers used symbols to bind their community together. One of the most iconic symbols that has persisted in Mormon culture is the beehive.[1] The beehive was described in *Deseret News* as such: "The hive and honeybees form our communal coat of arms. It is a significant representation of the industry, harmony, order, and frugality of the people, and of the sweet results of their toil, union, and intelligent cooperation."[2] It was through cooperation that the early pioneers created a community in a hostile environment. The beehive represents a community that persevered to keep Mormonism alive.

The beehive became the official emblem of the state of Utah on March 4, 1959.[3] Utah's official motto is, in fact, only one word, *industry*. Early pioneers had so few resources at their disposal that they had to rely on their hard work and industry to survive. Mormon pioneer values of hard work, industry, and perseverance are still found in the hearts and minds of Utahns and Mormons today.

The queer community, like the Mormon community, also has a history of using symbols to fortify and solidify our community as a unified whole. The rainbow has become the communal coat of arms for the queer community. The rainbow flag was originally designed by artist Gilbert Baker in 1978 after Harvey Milk, an influential gay leader, challenged Baker to create a symbol of the gay community.[4] Though the flag has gone through many revisions since then, and many other symbols have gained prominence in the queer community, the rainbow still persists as a symbol of queer celebration. Before the queer community, the rainbow was also used as a symbol of peace.[5] The variety of colors in the rainbow symbolize diversity within a cohesive union.

Combining the queer coat of arms with the Mormon coat of arms is an act of celebration in my identity as a queer Mormon. While there are many who claim that we cannot be both queer and Mormon, the rainbow beehive is a reminder that there are queer Mormons who rejoice in both identities and will not relinquish our authenticity to pessimists or patriarchs.

I see the passion and spirit of early Mormon pioneers shining through my fellow queer Mormons. I have participated in many queer Mormon groups, and I can tell you that we live and breathe the values of early Mormon pioneers. We are the pioneers of today, building a community with perseverance and industry in a hostile environment. Even when we were asked to leave churches and temples, we pressed forward. We picked up the pieces of shattered hopes in a celestial eternity and got to work. We did so frugally, on limited means. We buried our friends along the way. We lost far too many, but we carried on. We will march in the streets and sing in the pews. We will preach from pulpits with tears streaming down our cheeks. We have built a community worthy of a coat of arms.

If there were ever an anthem for the queer Mormon community, I imagine it would reflect the blazing relentlessness of the early Mormon pioneers and the burning flame of hope that all can be reconciled, even death. When I find myself losing hope in a better tomorrow for the queer Mormon community, I listen to the hymn "Come, Come Ye Saints." As a queer Mormon woman, a mother of three, a wife, a sister, a daughter, with nine generations of pioneers guiding my work, I hear these lyrics with new vigor! I hear the roaring voices of The Tabernacle

Choir at Temple Square singing "All is well!" with both melancholy and comfort. "All is well" is a proclamation of hope that even when all is not well, we can make it well through industry and perseverance. When I hear "Come, Come Ye Saints," I hear the queer Mormon's anthem.

> Come, come, ye Saints, no toil nor labor fear;
> But with joy wend your way.
> Though hard to you this journey may appear,
> Grace shall be as your day.
> 'Tis better far for us to strive
> Our useless cares from us to drive;
> Do this, and joy your hearts will swell—
> All is well! All is well!
>
> Why should we mourn or think our lot is hard?
> 'Tis not so; all is right.
> Why should we think to earn a great reward
> If we now shun the fight?
> Gird up your loins; fresh courage take.
> Our God will never us forsake;
> And soon we'll have this tale to tell—
> All is well! All is well!
>
> We'll find the place which God for us prepared,
> Far away in the West,
> Where none shall come to hurt or make afraid;
> There the Saints will be blessed.
> We'll make the air with music ring,
> Shout praises to our God and King;
> Above the rest these words we'll tell—
> All is well! All is well!
>
> And should we die before our journey's through,
> Happy day! All is well!
> We then are free from toil and sorrow, too;
> With the just we shall dwell!
> But if our lives are spared again
> To see the Saints their rest obtain,
> Oh, how we'll make this chorus swell—
> All is well! All is well!
>
> —William Clayton, 1814–1879

May we be the body of Christ and celebrate our diversity and unity. May we be like the honeybees and build a community together. May we be like the pioneers and never forsake hope in a better tomorrow. May we work in intelligent cooperation and rejoice in the sweet results of our toil. May we embrace our divine nature and make room for God's queerest children in our heavenly visions. May we use our priesthood power to act in the name of God. For with God, love wins.

Acknowledgements

Thank you Michael for being a superb editor.
Thank you Alexandria for molding this book into a cohesive story.
Thank you Steven for your insights into the biology of gender.
Thank you Taylor for introducing me to queer theology.
Thank you Lisa for helping me develop the tools to flourish.
Thank you Michaelann for your friendship and brilliant mind.
Thank you Lincoln for showing a better vision of Mormonism.
Thank you Brooke and Breann for your support and sisterhood.
Thank you Drew for being my partner, friend, lover, and salvation.
Thank you to my three children for teaching me unconditional love.
Thank you to all my queer peers for taking this journey with me.

Notes

Introduction

1. Dieter F. Uchtdorf, "Come, Join with Us!," General Conference, October 2013. https://www.churchofjesuschrist.org/study/general-conference/2013/10/come-join-with-us
2. Letter from Joseph Smith to Isaac Galland, Mar. 22, 1839, Liberty Jail, Liberty, Missouri, published in *Times and Seasons*, Feb. 1840, pp. 53–54.
3. 1 Peter 2:9

Chapter 1: Concerning Theology

1. Anthony Slagle, "In Defense of Queer Nation: From Identity Politics to a Politics of Difference," *Western Journal of Communication*.59, no. 2 (1995): 85–102, doi: 10.1080/10570319509374510.
2. Merrill Perlman, "How the word queer was adopted by the LGBTQ Community," *Columbia Journalism Review*, January 22, 2019. https://www.cjr.org/language_corner/queer.php
3. Peter 2:9–10
4. Russell M. Nelson, "The Correct Name of the Church," General Conference, October 2018.

5. Russell M. Nelson, "The Correct Name of the Church," General Conference, October 2018.
6. Doctrine and Covenants 135:6
7. Joseph Smith, *History of the Church*, 3:296–98.
8. Don Bradley, "The Grand Fundamental Principles of Mormonism," *Sunstone Magazine*, April 2006. pp. 32–41.
9. Gordon B. Hinckley, "Mormon Should Mean 'More Good,'" General Conference, October 1990.
10. Doctrine and Covenants 115:4
11. Russell M. Nelson, "The Correct Name of the Church," General Conference, October 2018.
12. "Style Guide—The Name of the Church," mormonnewsroom.org, 2020.
13. Jeffery R. Holland, "Helping Those Who Struggle with Same-Gender Attraction," General Conference, October 2007.
14. Patrick S. Cheng, *Radical Love: An Introudction to Queer Theology* (New York: Seabury Books, 2011),.p 19.
15. Moroni 10:5; 2 Nephi 32:5
16. Joseph Fielding Smith, *Doctrines of Salvation*, ed. Bruce R. McConkie, 3 vols. (1954–56), 1:48.
17. Articles of Faith 1:6.
18. Joseph Smith, *History of the Church*, 5:265.
19. Doctrine and Covenants 1:38
20. Doctrine and Covenants 26:2
21. Joan Roughgarden, *Evolution's Rainbow: Diversity, Gender, and Sexuality in Nature and People* (Oakland: University of California Press, 2013).
22. George Q. Cannon, *The Life of Joseph Smith, the Prophet*, 1888, p. 189.
23. Letter from Joseph Smith to Isaac Galland, Mar. 22, 1839, Liberty Jail, Missouri
24. Words: Jaclyn Thomas Milne, b. 1949. Music: Carol Baker Black, b. 1951, "Search, Ponder, and Pray," *Children's Songbook*, 2000.
25. Marianne Holman Prescott, "Elder Ballard Tackles Tough Topics and Gives Timely Advice to Young Adults," Church News, November 2017. https://www.churchofjesuschrist.org/church/news/elder-ballard-tackles-tough-topics-and-gives-timely-advice-to-young-adults
26. *History of the Church*, 5:555; from a discourse given by Joseph Smith on Aug. 27, 1843, in Nauvoo, Illinois; reported by Willard Richards and William Clayton.
27. 1 Corinthians 12:11–27
28. Doctrine and Covenants 8:2–3
29. 1 Nephi 10:19
30. Joseph Smith, *Teachings of the Prophet Joseph Smith*. p. 328.
31. Doctrine and Covenants 18:18; Alma 5:46; Alma 7:16; Doctrine and Covenants 76:116.
32. Doctrine and Covenants 88:118
33. Articles of Faith 1:13

34. Doctrine and Covenants 58:26–27
35. Doctrine and Covenants 26:2
36. James 2:14–17

Chapter 2: Concerning God

1. Genesis 1:26; Peter 1:3–4; 2 Nephi 26:33
2. Romans 8:17
3. Doctrine and Covenants 131:7–8
4. Doctrine and Covenants 88:12
5. Doctrine and Covenants 50:24; John 17:22; 2 Corinthians 3:18
6. Matthew 25:40
7. Doctrine and Covenants 93:29
8. Moses 6:51
9. Joseph Smith Jr., "King Follett Sermon," April 7, 1844.
10. Genesis 3:22
11. Psalms 82:6
12. Doctrine and Covenants 121:28
13. Doctrine and Covenants 121:32
14. Joseph Smith Jr., "King Follett Sermon," April 7, 1844.
15. Doctrine & Covenants 130:22
16. Joseph Smith—History 1:17; Articles of Faith 1:1
17. David L. Paulsen and Martin Pulido, "'A Mother There': A Survey of Historical Teachings about Mother in Heaven," BYU *Studies* 50, no. 1 (2011): 70–97.
18. Doctrine and Covenants 131:2
19. Genesis 1:27
20. Dallin H. Oaks, "The Keys and Authority of the Priesthood," General Conference, April 2014. "We are not accustomed to speaking of women having the authority of the priesthood in their Church callings, but what other authority can it be? When a woman—young or old—is set apart to preach the gospel as a full-time missionary, she is given priesthood authority to perform a priesthood function. The same is true when a woman is set apart to function as an officer or teacher in a Church organization under the direction of one who holds the keys of the priesthood. Whoever functions in an office or calling received from one who holds priesthood keys exercises priesthood authority in performing her or his assigned duties."
21. Joseph Smith Jr., "King Follett Sermon," April 7, 1844.
22. Ibid.
23. Romans 8:16–17
24. Doctrine and Covenants 93:36
25. Doctrine and Covenants 93:28–30; 88:118
26. Genesis 3:22
27. Isaiah 28:10; 2 Nephi 28:30; D&C 93:11–13

28. Doctrine and Covenants 130:18–19
29. Doctrine and Covenants 93:30
30. John 4:16
31. John 4:7–8
32. Matthew 22:36–40
33. 1 Corinthians 12
34. John 13:34–35
35. Matthew 25:40
36. Romans 12:5; 1 Corinthians 12: 12–27
37. Luke 6:27
38. Matthew 5:44
39. Doctrine and Covenants 6:6
40. John 4:18
41. Romans 12:3
42. Joseph Smith Jr., "King Follet Sermon," April 7, 1844, "When we understand the character of God, and know how to come to Him, he begins to unfold the heavens to us, and to tell us all about it. When we are ready to come to him, he is ready to come to us."
43. Acts 10:34; Romans 2:11; 2 Nephi 26:33
44. Romans 12:16
45. Moses 7:18
46. Colossians 3:14–16; Mormon 7:48; Mormon 7:46; 1 Corinthians 13:8; 1 Corinthians 16:14
47. Matthew 22:36–40
48. Matthew 5:17
49. Joseph Smith Jr., *History of The Church of Jesus Christ of Latter-day Saints*, 7 volumes, edited by Brigham H. Roberts (Salt Lake City: Deseret Book, 1957), 5:265.
50. L. Tom Perry, "Why Marriage and Family Matter—Everywhere in the World," General Conference, April 2015. https://www.churchofjesuschrist.org/study/general-conference/2015/04/why-marriage-and-family-matter-everywhere-in-the-world
51. Todd D. Christofferson, "Elder Christofferson Provides Context on Handbook Changes Affecting Same-Sex Marriages," YouTube, November 6, 2015. https://www.youtube.com/watch?v=iEEMyc6aZms
52. 2 Nephi 2:25; Moses 1:39
53. Benjamin Knoll, "Youth Suicide Rates and Mormon Religious Context: An Additional Empirical Analysis," *Dialogue: A Journal of Mormon Thought* 49, no. 2, Summer (2016): 25–44.
54. Doctrine and Covenants 58: 27–29
55. 1 Corinthians 13:8–10
56. Marianne Holman Prescott, "Elder Ballard Tackles Tough Topics and Gives Timely Advice to Young Adults," Church News, November 2017. https://www.churchofjesuschrist.org/church/news/elder-ballard-tackles-tough-topics-and-gives-timely-advice-to-young-adults
57. Doctrine and Covenants 58:26

58. Doctrine and Covenants 58:27
59. Articles of Faith 1:11; Doctrine & Covenants 64:34
60. 1 John 4:8
61. Matthew 5:48
62. 2 Nephi 2:25
63. Joseph Smith, *Teachings of the Prophet Joseph Smith*, pg. 255.
64. Alma 42:8
65. Moses 1:39
66. Matthew 5:48
67. Psalms 82:6; Doctrine and Covenants 132:24; LDS Gospel Topics Essays, "Becoming Like God," https://www.churchofjesuschrist.org/study/manual/gospel-topics-essays/becoming-like-god
68. John 14:3
69. Joseph Smith Jr., "King Follett Sermon," April 7, 1844.
70. Romans 8:16–17
71. Eliza R. Snow, "Let Us Cultivate Ourselves," Salt Lake City Seventeenth Ward Relief Society, February 18, 1869, chap. 10 in *At the Pulpit: 185 Years of Discourses by Latter-Day Saint Women*, ed. Jennifer Reeder and Kate Holbrook (Salt Lake City: The Church Historian's Press, 2017), 41–45.
72. Mattie Horne Tingey, "The School of Experience," World's Congress of Representative Women, Art Institute of Chicago, May 19, 1893, chap. 21 in *At the Pulpit: 185 Years of Discourses by Latter-Day Saint Women*, ed. Jennifer Reeder and Kate Holbrook (Salt Lake City: The Church Historian's Press, 2017), 83–87.
73. Sarah M. Kimball, "Our Sixth Sense, or the Sense of Spiritual Understanding," National Council of Women, Metzerott's Music Hall, Washington, DC, February 21, 1895, chap. 22 in *At the Pulpit: 185 Years of Discourses by Latter-Day Saint Women*, ed. Jennifer Reeder and Kate Holbrook (Salt Lake City: The Church Historian's Press, 2017), 89–92.
74. D. Todd Christofferson, "Why Marriage, Why Family," *Ensign*, May 2015, pg. 52. https://www.lds.org/general-conference/2015/04/why-marriage-why-family
75. Dallin H. Oaks, "Apostasy and Restoration," *Ensign*, May 1995, pg. 87. https://www.lds.org/general-conference/1995/04/apostasy-and-restoration
76. Gordon B. Hinckley, "And the Greatest of These is Love," *Ensign*, March 1984, pg. 87. https://speeches.byu.edu/talks/gordon-b-hinckley_greatest-of-these-love/
77. Boyd K. Packer, *Let Not Your Heart Be Troubled*, Bookcraft Inc, 1991, pp. 289–290.
78. Jeffery R. Holland, "Arizona Devotional for Young Single Adults," YouTube, April 26, 2016. https://www.youtube.com/watch?v=K4_LcENySzQ
79. Moses 4:3
80. 2 Nephi 2:27
81. Alma 29:4–5; 3 Nephi 28: 9–10
82. Doctrine and Covenants 137:9
83. James 2:17–18, 20, 26
84. Doctrine and Covenants 137:9

85. Moses 4:3
86. Roman 12:5; Corinthians 12
87. M. Russell Ballard, "The Doctrine of Inclusion," General Conference, October 2001. https://www.lds.org/general-conference/2001/10/doctrine-of-inclusion
88. Doctrine and Covenants 78:7
89. Doctrine and Covenants 88:18–20

Chapter 3: Concerning Christ

1. Joseph Smith, Teachings of the Prophet Joseph Smith, pg. 121.
2. Romans 8:17
3. 2 Nephi 9:12
4. Doctrine and Covenants 88:6
5. Luke 22:44
6. Luke 23:2, 14
7. John 18:38
8. John 19:1–3
9. John 19:4
10. John 19:6
11. Matthew 27:16
12. Matthew 27:24
13. Luke 23:33
14. John 19:11
15. John 6:51
16. Matthew 26:28
17. John 1:7 KJV
18. 2 Nephi 9:7
19. 1 Corinthians 12
20. David Basden, "Christ has no body now on earth but yours," (SSAA, a cappella), YouTube, Dec 10, 2015, https://www.youtube.com/watch?v=x6QEw0KtxJ8
21. 1 Corinthians 12
22. 1 Corinthians 12:14–22
23. 1 Corinthians 12:22
24. Acts 10:34; 2 Nephi 26:33
25. 1 Corinthians 12:25
26. Romans 15:12
27. John 13:34
28. Dieter F. Uchtdorf, "Four Titles," General Conference, April 2013.
29. James 2:26
30. Mark 14:22
31. Doctrine and Covenants 20:77, 79
32. Matthew 26:38, 42

33. Matthew 26:37
34. Moroni 7:46–47
35. Moroni 7:48
36. James Brooke, "Gay Man Dies From Attack, Fanning Outrage and Debate," *The New York Times*, October 12, 1998.
37. Julie Bindel, "The truth behind America's most famous gay-hate murder," *The Guardian*, October 25, 2014.
38. Jim Hughes, "Wyoming bicyclist recalls tragic discovery," *The Denver Post*, October 15, 1998, pg. A01.
39. "The Crucifixion of Matthew Shepard," *Vanity Fair*, March 1999. https://www.vanityfair.com/news/1999/13/matthew-shepard-199903
40. Deryn Guest et al., *The Queer Bible Commentary* (London: SCM Press, 2011).
41. Terrance McNally, *Corpus Christi*, 1999.
42. Romans 6:9
43. 1 Corinthians 15:22
44. Alma 40:23
45. 1 Corinthians 15:54–58
46. Moses 1:39
47. Matthew 10:7–8
48. John 14:12
49. John 11:14, 17
50. John 11:25
51. John 14:12
52. John 11:43–44

Chapter 4: Concerning The Family

1. M. Russell Ballard, "Doctrine of Inclusion," General Conference, October 2001.
2. 1 Corinthians 12:22
3. First Presidency and Council of the Twelve Apostles, "The Family: A Proclamation to the World," 1995.
4. Ibid.
5. Ibid.
6. Joseph Smith, Jr., "The King Follett Discourse," April 7, 1844.
7. Exodus 3:2 KJV; Matthew 3:16 KJV; 1 Timothy 1:17 KJV
8. David L. Paulsen and Martin Pulido, "'A Mother There': A Survey of Historical Teachings about Mother in Heaven," *BYU Studies* 50, no. 1 (2011): 70–97.
9. Genesis 1:27
10. Genesis 1:3–5
11. Genesis 1:5
12. Psalms 82:6; Romans 8:17; Romans 2:11

13. Alma 7:16; Alma 5:46; Doctrine and Covenants 76:116; Doctrine and Covenants 55:1; Alma 5: 54
14. Doctrine and Covenants 6:14–15; 2 Nephi 32:5
15. John 14:26; Doctrine and Covenants 130:22
16. 1 Corinthians 6:19–20
17. 2 Nephi 26:11
18. Doctrine and Covenants 88:15; Abraham 5:7
19. Helaman 14:30–31; 2 Nephi 2:27; Moses 7:32
20. *Teachings of the Prophet Joseph Smith*, sel. Joseph Fielding Smith (Salt Lake City: Deseret Book Company, 1938), p. 181.
21. Doctrine and Covenants 93:33–34
22. 2 Nephi 2:25
23. 2 Corinthians 3:18
24. Doctrine and Covenants 6:22–23

Chapter 5: Concerning Sexuality and Creation

1. Doctrine and Covenants 131:1–4
2. "Fertility Treatments," §38.6.9 in *General Handbook: Serving in The Church of Jesus Christ of Latter-Day Saints* (Salt Lake City: The Church of Jesus Christ of Latter-day Saints, December 2020).
3. Genesis 1:28
4. Abraham 3
5. "Fertility Treatments," §38.6.9 in *General Handbook: Serving in The Church of Jesus Christ of Latter-Day Saints* (Salt Lake City: The Church of Jesus Christ of Latter-day Saints, December 2020).
6. Ian Sample, "Three-parent babies explained: what are the concerns and are they justified?," *The Guardian*, February 2, 2015.
7. Ethics of surrogacy can be complicated and have often come at the expense of women of color. Consent and care of the surrogate is of supreme importance. Keep in mind, the technology of surrogacy itself is not immoral even if a specific application is immoral.
8. Fox News, "Grandmother Acting as Surrogate Delivers Healthy Granddaughter," *Fox News*, January 7, 2016.
9. NPR International, "A First: Uterus Transplant Gives Parents a Healthy Baby," *NPR International*, October 4, 2014.
10. James R. Clark, "Messages of the First Presidency of The Church of Jesus Christ of Latter-day Saints," 6 vols. (1965–75), pp. 6:178; Russell M. Nelson, "Our Sacred Duty to Honor Women," General Conference, April 1999.
11. M. Russell Ballard, "Daughters of God," General Conference, April 2008. https://www.lds.org/general-conference/1991/10/daughters-of-god
12. First Presidency and Council of the Twelve Apostles, "The Family: A Proclamation to the World," 1995.

13. Mark 10: 13–16; Matthew 19: 13–14; Luke 18:15–17
14. Guy Ringler, "Get Ready for Embryos from Two Men or Two Women," TIME, March 18, 2015. http://time.com/3748019/same-sex-couples-biological-children/
15. Blaire Ostler, "How a Mother Became a Transhumanist," June 6, 2015. http://www.blaireostler.com/journal/2015/6/6/how-a-mother-became-a-transhumanist
16. "Children Conceived by Artificial Insemination or In Vitro Fertilization," §38.4.2.7 in *General Handbook: Serving in The Church of Jesus Christ of Latter-Day Saints* (Salt Lake City: The Church of Jesus Christ of Latter-day Saints, December 2020).
17. Britni De La Cretaz. "What's it like to Chestfeed? The many obstacles trans men and other transmasculine people run into when feeding infants," *The Atlantic*, August 23, 2016. https://www.theatlantic.com/health/archive/2016/08/chestfeeding/497015/
18. Tamar Reisman and Zil Goldstein, "Case Report: Induced Lactation in a Transgender Woman," *Transgender Health* 3, no. 1 (May 2018): 24–26, doi:10.1089/trgh.2017.0044.
19. "Children Who Are Not Born in the Covenant," §38.4.2.2 in *General Handbook: Serving in The Church of Jesus Christ of Latter-Day Saints* (Salt Lake City: The Church of Jesus Christ of Latter-day Saints, December 2020).
20. Ezra Taft Benson, *Sermons and Writings of President Ezra Taft Benson*, Church of Jesus Christ of Latter-day Saints, 2003. pg. 216.
21. Taylor Petrey, "Toward a Post-Heterosexual Mormon Theology," *Dialogue: A Journal of Mormon Thought*. 44, no. 4 (Winter 2011).
22. Taylor Petrey, "Rethinking Mormonism's Heavenly Mother," *Harvard Theological Review* 109, no 3 (July 2016): 315–341, doi:10.1017/s0017816016000122
23. Taylor Petrey, "Toward a Post-Heterosexual Mormon Theology," *Dialogue: A Journal of Mormon Thought* 44, no. 4 (Winter 2011).
24. Mosiah 3:8; Moses 2:1; Genesis 2:21–23
25. Luke 1:34–35
26. Matthew 1:25
27. 1 Nephi 11:13–20; Alma 7:10
28. Brigham Young, "Character of God and Christ, etc.," July 8, 1860, *Journal of Discourses*, 8:115. "... there is no act, no principle, no power belonging to the Deity that is not purely philosophical. The birth of the Savior was as natural as are the births of our children; it was the result of natural action. He partook of flesh and blood—was begotten of his Father, as we were of our fathers." Bruce R. McConkie, *Mormon Doctrine*, 2nd edition, (Salt Lake City: Bookcraft, 1966), 822. "Our Lord is the only mortal person ever born to a virgin, because he is the only person who ever had an immortal Father. Mary, his mother, "was carried away in the Spirit" (1 Ne. 11:13–21), was "overshadowed" by the Holy Ghost, and the conception which took place "by the power of the Holy Ghost" resulted in the bringing forth of the literal and personal Son of God the Father. Christ is not the Son of the Holy Ghost, but of the Father (*Doctrines of Salvation*, vol. 1, pp. 18–20). Modernistic teachings denying the virgin birth are utterly and completely apostate and false."
29. 1 Corinthians 12:21–24

30. Moses 1:39
31. 2 Nephi 11:7
32. 1 Corinthians 12:27
33. Joseph Smith, *Teachings of the Prophet Joseph Smith*, pp. 353–54.
34. Doctrine and Covenants 131:1–4
35. Joseph Smith, *Teaching of the Prophet Joseph Smith*, pp. 300–301.

Chapter 6: Concerning Polygamy

1. Doctrine and Covenants 132
2. Hulda Cordelia Thurston Smith, "O My Children and Grandchildren," *Nauvoo Journal* 4, no. 2 (Fall 1992).
3. Todd Compton, *In Sacred Loneliness* (Salt Lake City: Signature Books, 1997), pp. 25–42.
4. Topical Essays, "Plural Marriage and Families in Early Utah," The Church of Jesus Christ of Latter-day Saints. https://www.churchofjesuschrist.org/study/manual/gospel-topics/plural-marriage-and-families-in-early-utah
5. Russell M. Nelson, "Revelation for our Church, Revelation for Our Lives," Gender Conference, 2018. https://www.lds.org/general-conference/2018/04/revelation-for-the-church-revelation-for-our-lives
6. "Sealing of a Man and Woman," §38.4.1 in *General Handbook: Serving in The Church of Jesus Christ of Latter-Day Saints* (Salt Lake City: The Church of Jesus Christ of Latter-day Saints, December 2020).
7. Doctrine and Covenants 132:20
8. Doctrine and Covenants 132:21
9. Brigham Young, *Journal of Discourses*, 11:269, Aug. 19, 1866.
10. Ibid.
11. Wilford Woodruff, *Wilford Woodruff's Journal*, 9 vols., ed., Scott G. Kenny (Salt Lake City: Signature Books, 1985), 6:527 (journal entry dated Feb. 12, 1870). "I attended the school of the prophets. Brother John Holeman made a long speech upon the subject of Polygamy. He Contended that no person Could have a Celestial glory unless He had a plurality of wives. Speeches were made By L. E. Harrington O Pratt Erastus Snow, D Evans J. F. Smith Lorenzo Young. President Young said there would be men saved in the Celestial Kingdom of God with one wife with Many wives & with No wife at all."
12. Woodruff, *Wilford Woodruff's Journal*, 7:31, journal entry dated Sept. 24, 1871.
13. Doctrine and Covenants 38:24–27; 4 Nephi 1:3; Moses 7:8
14. The Church of Jesus Christ of Latter-day Saints, "Plural Marriage in Kirkland and Nauvoo," Oct. 2014, https://www.lds.org/topics/plural-marriage-in-kirtland-and-nauvoo "The revelation on marriage required that a wife give her consent before her husband could enter into plural marriage. Nevertheless, toward the end of the revelation, the Lord said that if the first wife 'receive not this law'—the command to practice plural marriage—the husband would be "exempt from the law of Sarah," presumably

the requirement that the husband gain the consent of the first wife before marrying additional women."

15. Doctrine and Covenants 132: 61–63
16. Doctrine and Covenants 132: 64–65
17. Todd Compton, *In Sacred Loneliness* (Salt Lake City: Signature Books, 1997), pp. 15–16.
18. Emily Dickenson, "My Life Closed Twice Before its Close (96)," 1830–1886.
19. Matthew 22: 36–40; John 4:16
20. John 4:7–8

Chapter 7: Concerning Policy

1. "Prejudice," §38.6.14 in *General Handbook: Serving in The Church of Jesus Christ of Latter-Day Saints* (Salt Lake City: The Church of Jesus Christ of Latter-day Saints, December 2020).
2. Blaire Ostler, "Heavenly Mother: The Mother of All Women." *Dialogue: A Journal of Mormon Thought* 51, no. 4 (Winter 2018): 171–181.
3. John A. Widtsoe, *Priesthood and Church Government*, Deseret Book, 1954.
4. Doctrine and Covenants 84:19
5. John Taylor, *Millennial Star*, Volume 9, pg. 321.
6. John A. Widtsoe, *Program of the Church*, John Widtsoe, pg. 127.
7. Moses 1:39
8. Alma 13:8–9
9. 1 Corinthians 12:27
10. Joseph Smith, *Teachings of the Prophet Joseph Smith*, pg. 364.
11. Abraham 1:4
12. Abraham 1:2
13. *Church Handbook of Instructions*, §16.13. November, 2015.
14. *Church Handbook of Instructions*, §6.7.3. November, 2015.
15. Sarah Jane Weaver, "Treat Children with 'Utmost Respect and Love,' Writes The First Presidency in Letter regarding Same-Sex Marriage Policy," *Church News*, November 13, 2015. https://www.thechurchnews.com/archives/2015-11-13/treat-children-with-utmost-respect-love-writes-the-first-presidency-in-letter-regarding-same-sex-marriage-policy-29855
16. Ibid.
17. Alma 34:33–35
18. The First Presidency, "First Presidency Shares Messages from General Conference Leadership Session," *Church Newsroom*, April 4, 2019. https://newsroom.churchofjesuschrist.org/article/first-presidency-messages-general-conference-leadership-session-april-2019
19. Jamie Scot, "Shock the Gay Away: Secrets of Early Gay Aversion Therapy Revealed," *HuffPost*, June 2013.

20. Simon LeVay, *Queer Science: The Use and Abuse of Research into Homosexuality* (Cambridge: MIT Press, 1996), pp. 74, 109.

21. Douglas C. Haldeman, "Gay Rights, Patient Rights: The Implications of Sexual Orientation Conversion Therapy," *Professional Psychology: Research and Practice* 33, no. 3 (June 2002): 260–64, doi:10.1037/0735-7028.33.3.260.

22. David B. Cruz, "Controlling Desires: Sexual Orientation Conversion and the Limits of Knowledge and Law," *Southern California Law Review* 72, no. 5 (1999): 1297–1400.

23. American Academy of Pediatrics Committee on Adolescence, "Homsexuality and Adolescence," *Pediatrics* 92, no. 4 (October 1993). http://pediatrics.aappublications.org/content/92/4/631.full.pdf

24. Hilary Daniel and Renee Butkus, "Lesbian, Gay, Bisexual, and Transgender Health Disparities: Executive Summary of a Policy Position Paper from the American College of Physicians," *Annals of Internal Medicine* 163, no. 2 (July 2015): 135, doi:10.7326/m14-2482.

25. American Medical Association, "H-160.991 Health Care Needs of the Homosexual Population" (2012) http://www.ama-assn.org/ama/pub/about-ama/our-people/member-groups-sections/glbt-advisory-committee/ama-policy-regarding-sexual-orientation.page

26. American Psychoanalytic Association, "Position Statement on Attempts to Change Sexual Orientation, Gender Identity, or Gender Expression" (2012) http://www.apsa.org/content/2012-position-statement-attempts-change-sexual-orientation-gender-identity-or-gender

27. MAP Movement Advance Project. "Equality Maps: Conversion Therapy Laws." February 24, 2019. http://www.lgbtmap.org/equality-maps/conversion_therapy

28. "Church Continues to Oppose Conversion Therapy," *Church Newsroom*, October 2019. https://newsroom.churchofjesuschrist.org/article/statement-proposed-rule-sexual-orientation-gender-identity-change

29. Taylor G. Petrey, *Tabernacles of Clay: Sexuality and Gender in Modern Mormonism* (Chapel Hill: University of North Carolina Press, 2020).

30. Spencer W. Kimball, *Miracle of Forgiveness* (Salt Lake City: Bookcraft, 1969). pp. 77–85.

31. "Interview With Elder Dallin H. Oaks and Elder Lance B. Wickman: 'Same-Gender Attraction,'" *Church Newsroom*, 2006. https://newsroom.churchofjesuschrist.org/article/interview-oaks-wickman-same-gender-attraction

32. Doctrine and Covenants 131:1–3

33. Doctrine and Covenants 132:46

34. First Presidency and Council of the Twelve Apostles, "The Family: A Proclamation to the World," 1995.

35. Matthew 19:5–6 KJV

36. Matthew 5:27–28; Doctrine and Covenants 42:23–26; Doctrine and Covenants 59:6; 3 Nephi 12:27–28

37. Matthew 5:29–32

38. "Church Updates Temple Recommend Interview Questions," *Church Newsroom*, October, 2019. https://newsroom.churchofjesuschrist.org/article/october-2019-general-conference-temple-recommend

39. Doctrine and Covenants 20:77, 79

40. Matthew 22:40 KJV
41. 2 Nephi 2:25
42. Moses 1:39
43. Moses 4: 3–4
44. Camille West, "Church Updates Resources Addressing Same-Sex Attraction," *Church News*, October 25, 2016. https://www.churchofjesuschrist.org/church/news/church-updates-resources-addressing-same-sex-attraction
45. Quoted from video on the Church's *Mormon and Gay* website, accessed January 19, 2019. https://mormonandgay.churchofjesuschrist.org/
46. *Nauvoo Relief Society Minute Book*, 1842–1844, pp. 37–38.; "R.S. Reports: Pioneer Stake," 1905, pg. 14.
47. Russell M. Nelson, "A Plea to My Sisters," General Conference, October 2015.
48. Quentin L. Cook, "Church Updates Resources Addressing Same-Sex Attraction" Contributed by Camille West, October 25, 2016. https://mormonandgay.lds.org/videos?id=15209571875228076146#d.
49. Dieter F. Uchtdorf, "Transcript of President Dieter F. Uchtdorf's address to the Salt Lake City Inner City Mission," *Church Newsroom*, December 4, 2015. https://newsroom.churchofjesuschrist.org/article/president-uchtdorf-transcript-salt-lake-inner-city-mission

Afterword: Concerning the Beehive

1. Hal Cannon, *The Grand Beehive* (Salt Lake City: University of Utah Press, 1980).
2. Richard G. Oman, "Beehive Symbol," *Encyclopedia of Mormonism* (Macmillan Publishing Company, 1992).
3. "Utah State Flag and Seal," Pioneer: Utah's Online Library, State of Utah, February 23, 2019.
4. "MoMA Acquires the Rainbow Flag," MoMA.org. Museum of Modern Art, February 23, 2019. https://www.moma.org/explore/inside_out/2015/06/17/moma-acquires-the-rainbow-flag/
5. Devere Allen, "The Fight for Peace," *Political Science Quarterly*, 46, no. 4 (December, 1931): 611–613.

Blaire Ostler is a philosopher specialized in queer studies, and is a leading voice at the intersection of queer, Mormon, and transhumanist thought. She is also a board member and podcaster at Sunstone, and former CEO and board member at the Mormon Transhumanist Association. Blaire is also an artist and poet, and spends her spare time hiking, painting, writing, and bickering with her friends about almost any topic imaginable. Blaire lives in Utah with her husband and their three children.